S0-BZR-374

CHOMOLUNGMA

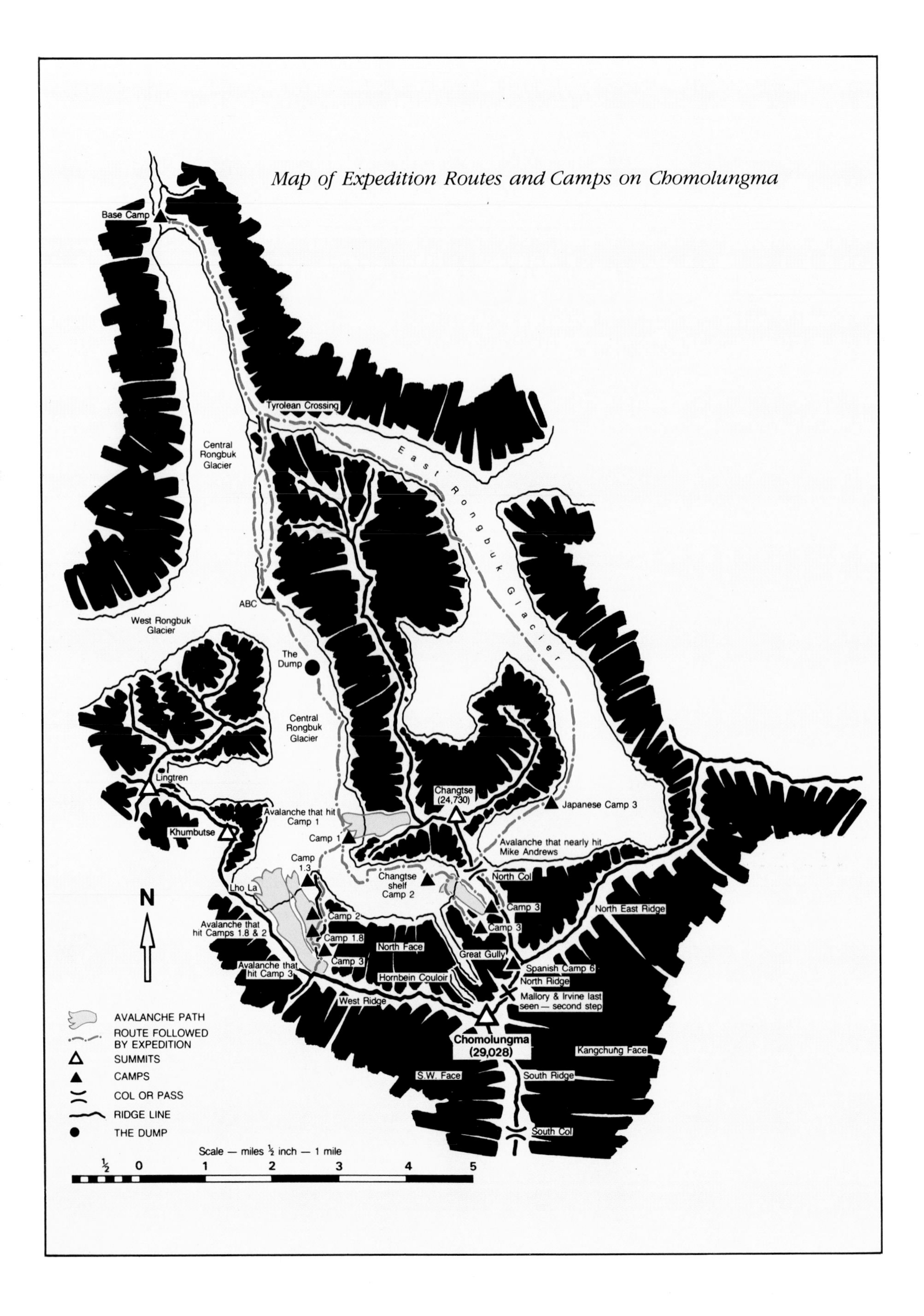

Map of Expedition Routes and Camps on Chomolungma
Base Camp
Tyrolean Crossing
Central Rongbuk Glacier
East Rongbuk Glacier
ABC
West Rongbuk Glacier
The Dump
Central Rongbuk Glacier
Lingtren
Khumbutse
Avalanche that hit Camp 1
Camp 1
Changtse (24,730)
Japanese Camp 3
Avalanche that nearly hit Mike Andrews
Camp 1.3
Changtse shelf Camp 2
North Col
Lho La
Camp 2
Camp 3
Camp 3
North East Ridge
Avalanche that hit Camps 1.8 & 2
Camp 1.8
North Face
Camp 3
Great Gully
Avalanche that hit Camp 3
Spanish Camp 6
North Ridge
Hornbein Couloir
Mallory & Irvine last seen — second step
West Ridge
N
AVALANCHE PATH
ROUTE FOLLOWED BY EXPEDITION
SUMMITS
CAMPS
COL OR PASS
RIDGE LINE
THE DUMP
Chomolungma (29,028)
Kangchung Face
S.W. Face
South Ridge
South Col
Scale — miles ½ inch — 1 mile
½ 0 1 2 3 4 5

CHOMOLUNGMA

New Zealanders on the North Face of Everest

GRAEME DINGLE & MIKE PERRY

HODDER AND STOUGHTON
AUCKLAND LONDON SYDNEY TORONTO

Other books by Graeme Dingle

Two Against the Alps
Wall of Shadows
The Seven Year Adventure
The Outdoor World of Graeme Dingle
First Across the Roof of the World (with Peter Hillary)
New Zealand Adventures (with Graham Mourie)

First published 1986.
ISBN 0 340 401117

Book design and typesetting by Acorn Graphics Ltd, Auckland.
Printed and bound in Hong Kong for Hodder and Stoughton Ltd, 44-46 View Road, Glenfield, Auckland, New Zealand.

Contents

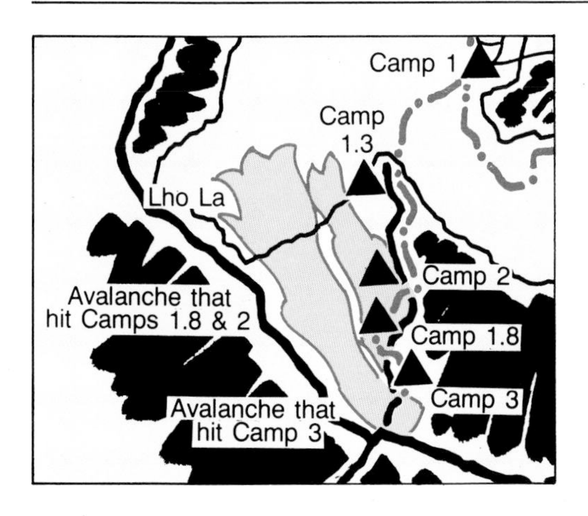

Hello ... this is ex-camp three calling.

When the avalanche buried camp three at 12.30 pm on 10 September 1985, the New Zealand team had been on Chomolungma for a month and the momentum of the ascent was just beginning to grow. We had consolidated a route to 24,000 feet and, given luck and a following wind, the first summit attempt would take place in two weeks.

This would be the culmination of four years' work since permission had been granted by the Chinese Mountaineering Association for a New Zealand expedition to the Chinese side of Chomolungma. Throughout those four years we had kept the dream alive despite the cynics. We had bludged food and equipment and trained. I have never trained so hard. Almost everyday I ran up the endless hills at the southern end of Lake Taupo, imposing on my mind and body pain and lung-bursting effort: over and over again I had imagined those last 2,000 feet to the summit of Chomolungma. I had even given up drinking alcohol, a sacrifice or penance that many thought was going a bit far and almost certainly the result of too much time spent in India.

But although of luck we arguably had sufficient, the following wind was absent. At 12.30 pm on 10 September my team, Toyota, were resting. Having just established camps two and three on the west spur, we had retreated down the mountain to recharge our batteries. Shaun Norman was still descending from advance base camp, Ross Cullen and I were feeding our faces in the base camp kitchen tent, and Rob Blackburne was squatting on the rustic 'john'. As Ross and I crammed another tasty morsel into our mouths Rob shambled into the tent

The avalanche, that halted the west ridge attempt, rolls across the Lho La towards Khumbutse. Four thousand feet above, Mike Rheinberger and Peter Allen are already running down the slide path to search for Warwick Anderson, Mike Perry and camp three — all vanished beneath the debris. (Dick Price)

pulling up his pants.

'There's been an avo on the spur,' he puffed. We ran out into the midday brightness and squinted up at Chomolungma 12 miles away. Near the top of the spur we could clearly see the smudge of a fresh avalanche. In a kind of numbed quiet we stared up muttering the occasional expletive.

'Radio,' someone suddenly whispered. I ran into the tent to get it, Ross got his telephoto lense and we stood amongst the graves and memorials to earlier victims of Chomolungma, on the moraine hillock above base camp, trying to piece together the disaster. Our leader, Austin Brookes, was at camp one with Steve Bruce watching the drama through a telescope. In a fearful but cool tone he soon began to describe the scene over the radio.

'A huge avalanche has come down from the ridge ... part of it went right across the Lho La and 500 feet up Khumbutse ... there are two people digging so presumably two people are buried ... I think there's someone lying in a sleeping bag.' We all felt the chill hand of fear bristling our scalps as we contemplated the

Silhouetted against the summit, Warwick Anderson descends to camp two on the west ridge after an afternoon spent repairing our avalanche-mangled fixed rope. Steve Bruce wrote in his diary: 'Climbing the spur is like climbing an entirely separate mountain. As you look across at the upper slopes of Chomolungma, it is difficult to feel that you are part of an attempt to climb it, we seem so far removed.'

loss of some of our friends.

Peter Allen was one of those at camp three. He describes the events leading up to the avalanche:

> *The day before the avo we had climbed from camp two to camp three, the first team up here since the avalanche and storm that trapped Team Toyota at camp two. That avalanche had stripped all the ground below camp one-point-eight down to a hard surface and the fixed rope was stretched taut for several hundred feet, with the old anchors hanging from it. Camp one-point-eight was wrecked, the tent squashed flat and lying forlornly on a tiny ledge. The whole area where Dick and Hugh's snow cave had been was gone. Above the break which curved upward to the right, the snow was still soft and deep and the ropes were buried. Mike Perry led this section up to the end of the fixed ropes. It was very hot and the going was slow in knee-deep snow. At the end of the fixed*

Team Fairydown nears camp three on the west ridge. 'We were plugging up to knee- and thigh-deep through the most unstable snow I've ever been in. Spread out for safety, we toiled upwards with increasing disquiet. Progress was rather slow but we were constantly tensed for the desperate struggle that would ensue if the slope released.' (Warwick Anderson)

ropes I led out another 300 feet of rope. It took me an hour and ten minutes! We eventually reached camp three, thoroughly exhausted at 6.30 pm. Although both Mike Perry and I were concerned about the state of the snow it never seemed bad enough to warrant retreat. The next morning (the 10th) Mike Perry woke up suffering from an eye infection provoked by his contact lenses and could not see with that eye. The brightness had caused the other eye to go out in sympathy so he was effectively blind. Mike Rheinberger was very keen to push on up to the top of the west shoulder and out on to the west ridge. The crest of the ridge was about 500 to 600 feet above and Rheinberger wanted to traverse diagonally leftwards on to the low point of the ridge. I was still concerned about the state of the snow and we eventually agreed that Warwick should commence construction of a snow cave,

---

Mike Rheinberger and Peter Allen build a tent platform at camp three (west ridge). 'Camp three was situated beneath what was clearly a perfect example of a windslab slope; and our situation epitomised the desperate risks that climbers on Chomolungma find themselves taking. To turn back from that minefield of a slope was to abandon the climb. It was too early and we were too highly motivated to seriously consider that option. If we climbed directly up above the tents we might not avoid triggering an avalanche but would be in the best position to stay above the break-line. As it happened the events of the following day were even more grotesque than we had feared.' (Warwick Anderson)

---

a safer alternative to tents, while Rheinberger and I went up to the ridge on a reconnaissance.
Warwick started digging while Mike Perry lay in the VE 24 tent with his eyes covered. We set off upwards carrying a rope and (fortunately) a shovel. The snow was deep and bottomless. I dug holes but never found a sliding layer, so we plugged on up. I guess it took us an hour to an hour and a half until we were about 30 feet from the top. Rheinberger was in the lead and had veered a bit to the right when we hit a crusty layer. I was very worried and steered him straight up again. We were so close to the crest it seemed safer to press on — it was as well we did. I felt rather than heard the crack as the break shot in from the right just under Rheinberger's heels, shot down our track (between my legs) and then went right again a few feet lower down. I leaped to the safe ground on the right, thrust in my axe and looked below me. The whole slope was a sea of tumbling blocks as wide as my field of vision, surging down on camp three.
I screamed 'Warwick ... Warwick ... Warwick' till my lungs were empty, and then I saw Warwick run from the VE 24 to the snowcave with Perry hard on his heels. We watched aghast as the snow blocks tumbled over the camp.
A moment later we were running recklessly down the avalanche trail towards the camp. At first we thought that the avo had stopped at the camp because the blue Chrysalis tent and a red sleeping bag were on the surface, but when we arrived we found that the tent was just a wreck floating on the top of the debris. The problem now was that we didn't know how far it had been carried from the camp.
Rheinberger started digging in an obvious mound for no special reason other than it looked about the right place. I checked the sleeping bag which was empty and then started screaming Warwick's name again, looking despairingly across the sea of broken snow blocks and wondering how to find a reference point. Almost simultaneously Rheinberger called that the snow mound was the VE 24 (squashed flat) and then the tip of Warwick's red glove poked out of the snow 30 feet to the right. We dug quickly and soon had his head uncovered. We were greatly relieved to find that Perry was underneath him. They were both completely immobile so we first dug an airway down to Perry then dug them out.
Mike was pretty cold from his twenty-minute burial but otherwise they were okay.

Meanwhile, 7,000 feet below at base camp, we willed our eyes to see more clearly the tiny dots we could make out through Ross's telephoto lense.

'Camp one, this is base ... what can you see, Austin?'

'Okay, they're digging one person out ... now another ... they're still digging ... probably for the radio. ...'

Then another voice came on the air. It was Warwick, sounding happy, 'Hello ... this is ex-camp three calling.'

Team Fairydown, as those at camp three were called, had another problem now. The camp was wrecked so there was no doubt that they would have to descend, but much of the snow on the spur below was probably still in an awful condition and now that the immediate danger had passed every fibre of their bodies and minds called out for caution. They decided in the end to wait until late in the day and descend to camp two when things were a bit cooler.

At camp two, the crevasse camp or 'Pukerua', as we affectionately called it in Maori, Team Comalco had been preparing to move up to camp three. Now

---

Mike Perry describes his burial in the avalanche that halted the attempt on the west ridge: 'The sound of the slab break, when it came, at the end of a long morning's wait, was soft, understated, almost marvellous in the way its terminal message was so gently delivered. A frantic shout from Peter Allen, arriving a millisecond later, was utterly superfluous. Warwick and I were well advanced, at least mentally, in our lunge for survival. For me, it was easy: I was blind, so the decision was Warwick's. He dashed into the incipient snowcave and I followed, homing in on his voice. After the burial, we were immobile, but our heads were in a small air cavity. There would be company for the impending suffocation. The oxygen supply was clearly dwindling, and conversely, our panting was increasing. Time slowed down, badly. And then, it was over. First Warwick forced the tip of his glove to the surface — that sight of blue sky was like a blast of pure oxygen — and then, incredibly, the pinhole view of a grim-faced Peter Allen. Grim but a beautiful sight. Clambering to the surface a few minutes later, I was still grinning.' (Warwick Anderson)

encouraged by Austin to 'cool it', Bruce Farmer and his keen men, Dick Price, Hugh Van Noorden and Mike Andrews, were thrown into an unhappy state of indecision — to continue up in spite of the bad conditions or to descend and wait for the snow to improve?

Foremost in everyone's mind was the time left. It was already 10 September. Our first summit attempt was scheduled for 26 September (coincidentally also the day that Austin's wife Julie was due to have their baby). We had to get to the top by the end of the first week in October because regular as clockwork each year at that time violent storms lash the mountain and jet-stream winds come down to low levels, making progress high up virtually impossible. So realistically we had three weeks to get a team into position for a summit attempt and if, as we hoped, we were to get several people on top, we had a fortnight to get a top camp established. We were at a cross-roads — our mountaineering judgement was about to be put to the test and it was anyone's guess whether it or raw ambition would win.

Having just watched the life and death struggle at camp three, Austin was

Team Fairydown unearthing the wreckage of camp three. Mike Perry recalls, 'After the avalanche a kind of mist settled over the ridge, softening the disorder around the camp and dampening the reverberations of our recent trauma.'

determined that good judgement should prevail. No one wanted success more than he but above this he wanted everyone to return home. This is the crux of Himalayan climbing, and particularly on Chomolungma, sound judgement always jousting with ambition. What level of risk is the summit really worth?

To understand this question we need to take a look at our predecessors on the north side. Those people who were prepared to push beyond the known frontiers of the mountain, of technology and, perhaps closer to the heart of the question, of the body and the mind.

Long faces at camp two (west ridge). Bruce Farmer and Dick Price hear of the demise of camp three from Rheinberger. 'Pukerua' as camp two was known, featured a manic air-conditioning system: an unstoppable draught of frigid air from the depths of the crevasse vented directly on to the sleeping platform. (Warwick Anderson)

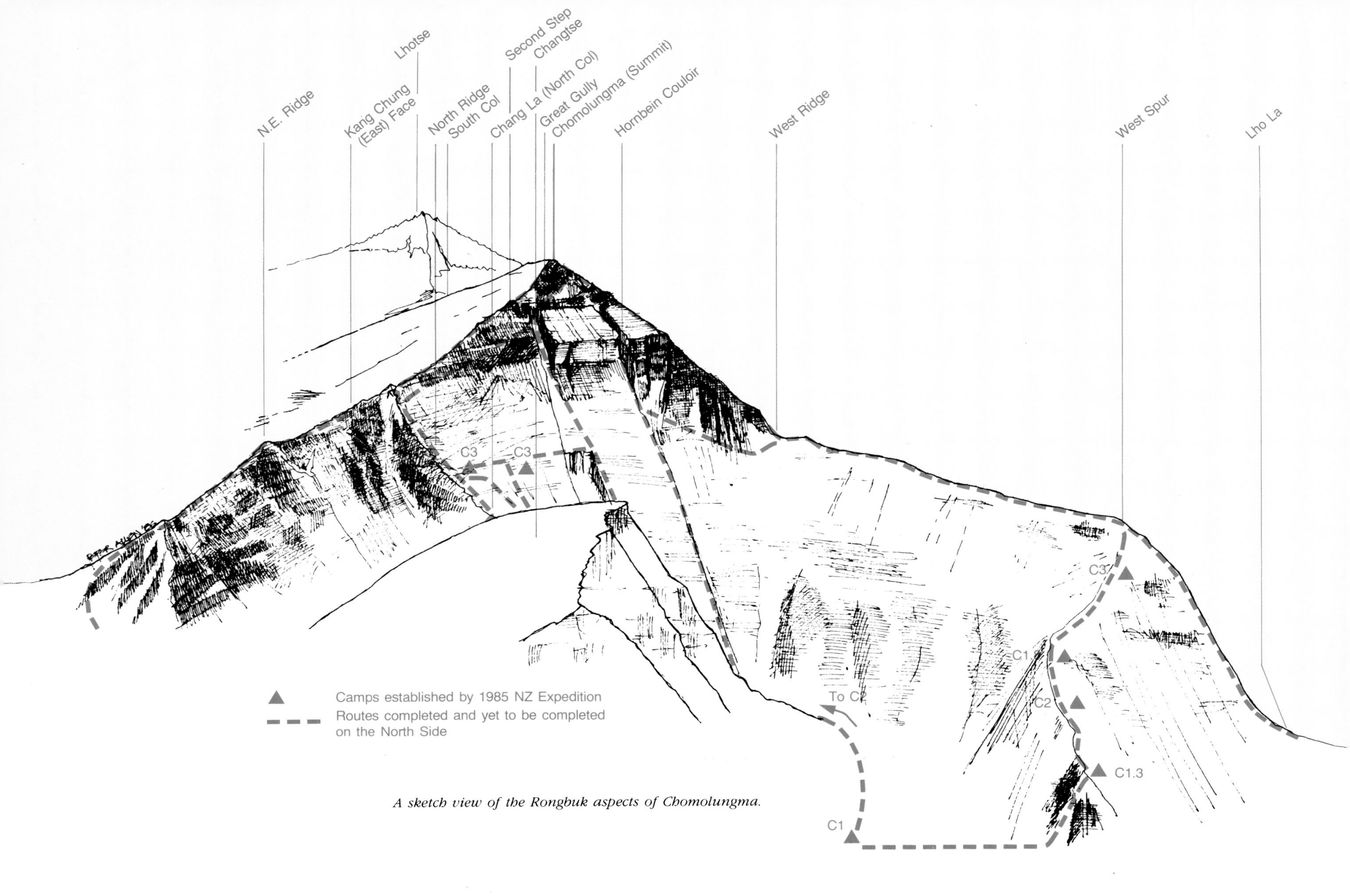

A sketch view of the Rongbuk aspects of Chomolungma.

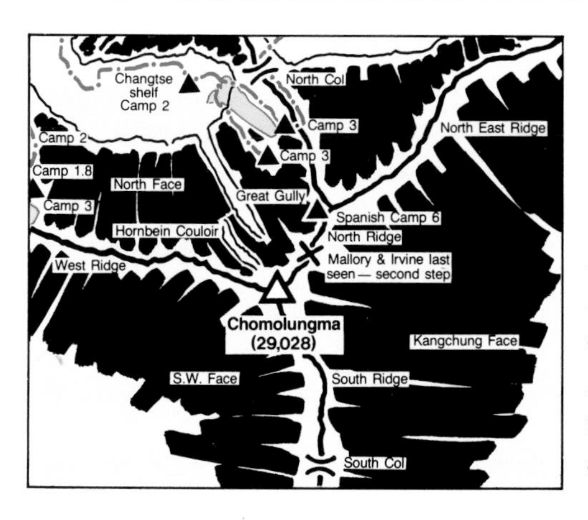

Above 27,000 feet, with the air pressure down to one third, only the toughest physical and mental specimen can operate effectively at all.

The epoch of Everest began as an exclusively British affair. This was not because other nations were not interested in the prize of the highest summit in the world. On the contrary, and when one of these nations, Switzerland, got the opportunity for an attempt in 1952 they almost beat the British to it. However, it was not to be and the British, who had struggled so hard for success for over thirty years, deservedly took the prize the following year when on 29 May 1953 two members of a British expedition, the New Zealander, Ed Hillary, and the Indo-Nepali, Tensing Norkay, reached the summit from the south at 11.30 am.

Until then all the British attempts had taken place from Tibet, which involved a long approach march from India and Sikkim, and therein lies the secret to the exclusivity. The British controlled India and in 1903 they decided to establish themselves in Tibet. They were concerned at the growing flirtation between Russia and the thirteenth Dalai Lama, which had the potential of bringing the Russians too close to their Indian borders. A force was sent under the command of Colonel Francis Younghusband with orders to march on Lhasa and to establish a consulate there. The advance was bitter and bloody and when they arrived in Lhasa they found that the Dalai Lama had fled to Mongolia. However a treaty was signed in September 1904 and the Russian threat never eventuated. Subsequent consuls were not always sympathetic to mountaineering ambitions, but the very presence of a British consul must have aided the cause considerably. The combination of this and British control of India was a very successful block to activity on Everest by other nationalities.

The first expeditions must have been incredibly interesting affairs. Nowadays

Twilight on Chomolungma, Goddess Mother of the Earth.

mountaineers can drive directly to base camp at 16,800 feet a few days after landing at Beijing Airport. The expeditions of the 1920s and 30s took months: journeying by train across Europe to the Middle East, then steaming by boat across the Indian Ocean to Bombay. From there it was train to Calcutta, then road to Darjeeling, the British hill station near the Indo-Sikkimese border. The trek would then begin in earnest, north through Sikkim over the Serpo La to Kampa Dzong on the wind-swept Tibetan plateau. The caravan of porters, yaks and sahibs would then continue westward for 155 miles to Tingri Dzong where there were hot springs to wash away the grime and the pains of the trek. From Tingri the track went north over an 18,000-foot pass to Rongbuk monastery, the highest in the world at 16,500 feet. The great value of the trek, however, was that expedition members became very fit and well acclimatised to the high altitudes before getting on to Everest. The disadvantage must have been that it was a hell of a long way home when one came off the mountain physically and mentally wrecked.

The task of the first expedition in 1921 was to find the easiest route on to the mountain. Nepal was closed so the long circuitous route through Sikkim was the only possibility. As the party approached across Tibet they would have seen the north ridge in profile and its easy angle must have filled them with hope. It seems, however, that this first trip was not a happy one. The leader was a crabbed Scot called Harold Raeburn who had been a great mountaineer, but by 1921 he was a little past it and was not very well from the outset. Hardly had the party crossed into Tibet when another member, Doctor Kellas, one of the most experienced Himalayan climbers of the time, died of a heart attack after a short illness.

This 1921 expedition was George Leigh Mallory's first Himalayan trip. He was a man stamped in the heroic mould, a product of the public school and raised to create a legend. Like Scott of the Antarctic and Lawrence of Arabia, Mallory was destined, almost against his wishes, to satisfy the British public's need for a hero on Everest. They needed this hero at any cost and in the end the account would be settled with Mallory's life. From the start of the 1921 escapade Mallory established himself as the psychological leader. There is no doubt that he went well at high altitude but I wonder at his general mountaineering sense, because despite his travels in the Rongbuk valley he completely missed the East Rongbuk that drains the eastern side of the North Col and later became the normal approach. Instead he took his party up a tributary of the Arun, the Kharta, and at the head of this valley they crossed the 22,350-foot-high Lhakpa La, descended 1,200 feet to the East Rongbuk and then climbed up to the North Col. This was as far as the party went that year and, although it seemed only a modest success, the way had been opened to the north ridge.

In 1922 Mallory was the only veteran of the first expedition to join the second expedition. Perhaps the outstanding aspect of this second expedition was the superb leadership by big jovial Englishman, Brigadier General Charles Granville Bruce. As a result it seems to have been a very happy expedition.

As long as people have attempted Everest there has been a continual argument about the ethics of using oxygen, and this expedition was no exception. There were to be two main attempts: the first without the 'English air' as the Sherpas called the oxygen and the second using it. On the first attempt Mallory took Howard Somerville and Edward Norton. They turned back at 26,800 feet. The second attempt was by the Australian scientist, George Finch, who had designed the oxygen equipment, and a cousin of the general, Geoffrey Bruce, who with true British eccentricity had never been mountaineering before. Finch was the first Australasian to attempt Everest. He was a tall, lean man whose ideas seem to have been a little before their time. He had failed the medical for the first British expedition in 1921 but went higher than anyone else in 1922. He was at the forefront of the development of oxygen equipment and used a self-made duvet jacket in 1922, more than a decade before they came into common use. It would appear that his rough and tough ways were not well liked by the 'public school mountaineers' of the time and, though he was clearly very competent, he found it difficult to get into Everest expeditions. Finch and Bruce reached 27,300 feet, an altitude record at that time, and had been climbing at nearly twice the rate of Mallory's party when a malfunction in Bruce's oxygen set forced them to turn back. As the expedition was building up to a third attempt, seven Sherpas were killed in an avalanche on the slopes of the North Col and this was the sad end to the second expedition.

Two years later the British were back. The British public wanted success this time and many feel that Mallory sensed his Waterloo. He had to get up or not bother coming back and the odds were heavily against success. Two thousand feet does not sound like much but near the limit of human capability it is an eternity. At sea level I can run up 2,000 feet in around thirty minutes, but above 27,000 feet, with the air pressure down to one third, only the toughest physical and mental specimen can operate effectively at all. It is like running an entire marathon on oxygen debt.

On this third expedition, Norton, from the 1922 expedition, reached 28,126 feet without oxygen. A few days later Mallory set out with Andrew Irvine, a relatively inexperienced mountaineer, whom Mallory liked. It has been suggested that Mallory chose Irvine as his companion because of physical attraction rather than his soundness as a mountaineer. They set out from their camp six on 8 June and climbed into history. They were last seen by Noel Odell on the crest of the north ridge at about 27,800 feet; the time was 12.50 pm.

Back in England many wanted to believe that they had reached the summit, that Mallory like Scott had heroically made it but died on the way back. Many experts were in no doubt that they had but, considering the time and their slow rate of ascent, this would seem unlikely. Anyway, it is all semantics: the aim of the game is to get back again.

It was not until 1933 that a new wave of British attempts on the north ridge began, but these expeditions fared no better than those of the 1920s. In 1933 three climbers, Percy Wyn Harris, Lawrence Wager and Frank Smythe, all reached the same height as Norton had in 1924 and this was the best that the 1930s could produce.

Perhaps the most extraordinary attempt on Everest took place in 1934, when

Maurice Wilson set out to prove that people could do anything if they set their minds to it. His intention was to learn to fly in England, fly out to India and Tibet, land as high on Everest as possible and walk to the top. It was, of course, a preposterous idea but surprisingly he did learn to fly, not very well perhaps, but one must admire his push, and despite all the authorities could do to stop him, he did manage to fly to India. There his Britannic Majesty's authorities finally grounded him, but undeterred, Wilson went to Darjeeling, hired Sherpas and trekked into Tibet in disguise. Sadly he knew little about mountaineering and it would seem even less about the workings of the body on a mountain. He ate very little and there is even one theory that he thought he could do it by fasting. Whatever the truth he made several brave attempts to reach the North Col and finally died of exhaustion in or near his camp at the head of the East Rongbuk. His body was found by Shipton's party the following year.

In 1935 Eric Shipton chose a New Zealand school teacher, Dan Bryant, to accompany the reconnaissance expedition of that year. This was perhaps one of the most successful Himalayan expeditions of all time because, although it did not get very high on Everest, team members climbed twenty-six peaks of over 20,000 feet. It was an orgy of exploration in keeping with Shipton's light, fast and efficient style.

They did not achieve much on Everest but there were two key factors that would contribute greatly to eventual success. One of their Sherpas was a young man called Tensing Norkay, on his own long road to great things. And although Dan Bryant did not acclimatise that well, his cheerfulness and keen nature made Shipton well disposed to New Zealanders, and it was partly as a result of this that he chose Ed Hillary and George Lowe for the successful 1953 expedition.*

Neither the 1936 nor the 1938 attempts got very high but on the latter trip Shipton and Bill Tilman led the first ascent of the western approach to the North Col, the same approach that we were to use forty-seven years later. And they found it no less dangerous than we did. Tilman commented, 'The sun, feeble though it was, had been on the slope for an hour and from its effect on the snow I felt it was high time for us to be off it.'

As Shipton and Tilman thankfully reached the relative safety of the North Col, they could not have known that this was the last time for many years that anyone would tread the northern slopes of Everest. For twenty-two years the great faces and glaciers would be the domain solely of the choughs and ravens, and it would be forty-two years before westerners stood on the North Col again. War and its aftermath consumed much of the world for the next decade, and almost

*The original 1953 expedition line-up had included three New Zealanders, the third being the legendary guide Harry Ayres. But when Shipton was sacked from the leadership position, the new leader, John Hunt, decided he did not want Ayres, apparently because he was a professional but possibly also he was feeling that two New Zealanders were quite sufficient antipodean representation in a mainly British show. Ed Hillary has said that he believes had Harry been included it would have been two New Zealanders on top to grace the new Queen's coronation.

At that time New Zealanders were British subjects but New Zealand citizens, so it was not until September 1975 that the first 'real' British climbers reached the summit when the Scot, Dougal Haston, and Englishman, Doug Scott, reached the top after climbing the south-west face.

immediately after this dark clouds gathered over Tibet. The Chinese takeover came in 1950 and ten years later the cultural revolution ravaged the country.

There is a strong rumour that the Russians, in an attempt to be the first to top Everest in 1952, lost six climbers high on the north face but this is unsubstantiated. What is known is that in 1958 the Chinese and Russians collaborated in a reconnaissance up to the head of the East Rongbuk. However, before the joint attempt could take place, the two nations fell out politically and only the Chinese made the attempt in 1960. By now the official name for Everest north of the border was the Chinese Qomolangma Feng; to the Tibetans it was still Chomolungma.

If you consider the experience of the group and the standard of equipment that was used, that first Chinese attempt was perhaps the most amazing ascent of Chomolungma ever made. Their story was so incredible that until quite recently western mountaineers simply did not believe it. This was assisted by the weird account written by Chinese journalists and the fact that no summit pictures had been taken. But pictures would have been impossible as they were on top during the night.

The first thing the expedition had to do was build a road to base camp, what

Base Camp for the 1924 British Everest expedition. Today the scene is virtually unchanged save for the proliferation of C.M.A. trucks and Toyota Landcruisers.
© Royal Geographical Society, London. Reproduced courtesy of Arthur Ellis and Co. Dunedin.

could be more logical — it only had to cross one 18,000-foot-high pass! After our expedition I spoke with Chu Ying-Hua, one of the successful summiters, and asked him if they had had any special problems approaching the mountain in 1960. He replied matter-of-factly, 'No special problems ... but we had to make the road.'

'How long did that take?' I asked.

'Oh ... about a year.'

Apart from this extraordinary beginning the build-up on the mountain went quite normally. The top camp was placed at 27,800 feet and on 24 May four men, Wang Fu-Cho, Gompa (a Tibetan), Chu Ying-Hua and Liu Lien-Man, set out at about 10 am for the summit. It took them two hours to reach the foot of the second step, the obstacle around which so much controversy revolved regarding whether or not Mallory and Irvine had climbed it before disappearing in 1924. The step was found to be 100 feet high and they climbed the first 90 feet without too much difficulty, but burdened with bulky down-suits, oxygen equipment and clumsy boots, they faltered below the head wall. Liu Lien-Man tried several times to climb the final 12 feet but each time he fell back exhausted. Finally Chu Ying-Hua removed his boots and using Liu Lien-Man's shoulders as a launching pad he managed to scrabble up the final few feet. The time was 5 pm, the second step had taken five hours to climb. They had probably unwittingly made the first and only pure ascent of the famous second step, as nowadays the feature is festooned with ropes and even a ladder and is likely to remain so.

At 28,500 feet Liu Lien-Man could go no further and sat down to await the return of the others. A little higher their oxygen ran out but they continued, often crawling on all fours. One gets an indication of just how exhausted they were in that it took them thirty minutes to climb one step on the ridge that was only 3 feet high. Finally at 4.20 am they reached the summit. They buried the bust of Chairman Mao that they had carried, collected some rock samples for their beloved leader, Mao, and started down. That is not the end of this remarkable story. Liu Lien-Man was still in good shape, having survived a night out higher than anyone before him, and what is more he had saved his oxygen for his mates, a gesture that reduced them to tears. Five days later they were back at the base camp, safe except for frost-bite. Chu Ying-Hua subsequently lost all his toes and some of his fingers.

A Chinese party once again reached the summit in the spring of 1975. This time the nine summiters included a Tibetan woman called Phantog, who missed being the first woman to the summit by a few days. (On 16 May Mrs Junko Tabei with a Japanese group had reached the top by the South Col route.)

Over a nine-month period in 1976 Zhou Enlai, Chu The and Mao Zedong all died. The triumvirate that had led China for nearly forty years had gone and almost immediately things began to loosen up. In February 1978 the Panchen Lama was suddenly released from Qin Chang Prison, and many other prisoners, the lucky few that had survived, were released in Tibet. The Chinese even invited the Dalai Lama back to take up his position at the head of the Tibetan people again. The western world had been mainly oblivious to Tibet's pain, however, and to many the most significant fact was that Tibet was open to tourists and mountaineers from all round the world for the first time in history.

In 1980 the doors of Tibet were opened (carefully) to foreign mountaineers. First on to Chomolungma was a Japanese Alpine Club team. Their expedition simultaneously attempted the north face and the north ridge. On 3 May Kato Yasuo stood alone on the summit after ascending the north ridge; a week later his success was shared by Ozaki Takashi and Omohiro Tsuneo. Their late-night arrival on the summit cost them dearly with severe frost-bite but a magnificent (and yet-to-be repeated) route, directly up the centre of the north face connecting with the Hornbein Couloir and thence to the summit, was complete.

No sooner had the Japanese gone than, almost inevitably, Reinhold Messner appeared on the scene. In total contrast to the Japanese, whose tactics had included the traditional mix of fixed rope, oxygen and many climbers, Messner attempted something that many mountaineers dreamed of but did not have the courage or vision to accomplish — a solo ascent of Chomolungma without artificial oxygen. With his long list of Himalayan ascents, capped in 1978 by the first ascent of Chomolungma without artificial oxygen, Messner was singularly well qualified for the task. With only one companion, Nena Ritchie Holgein, herself a dynamic and interesting lady of Peruvian and American parentage, Messner walked up the East Rongbuk valley towards the North Col. Nena waited at their camp in the head of the Rongbuk and from there Messner set out alone. He had intended to climb the north ridge but found that there was too much snow on the ridge in the monsoon season, so he traversed out on to the north face and into the Great Gully. Here conditions were a little better and with only one further camp he was able to reach the summit on 20 August 1980. I wonder what Mallory would have said; the modern mountaineering world simply looked on in stunned acknowledgement, tinged with a little jealousy.

The Japanese had established the hardest route on the north side in 1980, but harder still was to come. On 8 and 9 October 1983, six Americans, Carlos Buhier, Kim Momb, Louis Reichardt, Jay Cassell, George Lowe and Daniel Reid, reached the summit having climbed the last of Chomolungma's great faces, the extremely difficult 10,000-foot-high Kang Chung or east face.

For sheer courage, pushiness and luck, however, the prize must go to five Australians, Lincoln Hall, Tim Macartney-Snape, Greg Mortimer, Andy Henderson and Geoff Bartram, who pushed a bold new route up the central north face during the post-monsoon season of 1984. Just before they launched their final push, an avalanche buried most of their gear but they managed to scrounge sufficient replacement gear from their film crew (Macartney-Snape had to wear Nordic ski boots), and set off again, climbing a spur to the right of the Great Gully until at about 23,000 feet they were able to traverse into the Gully itself. At this point, the onset of cerebral oedema forced Geoff Bartram to descend. Their top camp was rather low, at 26,500 feet, and a late start on 3 October gave them little chance of reaching the summit. Hall was forced to turn back after a few hundred feet but the others plodded stoically on. Just as the sun dipped below the western horizon Macartney-Snape followed by Mortimer reached the top. Sadly, impending darkness forced Henderson to stop less than 200 feet below the summit.

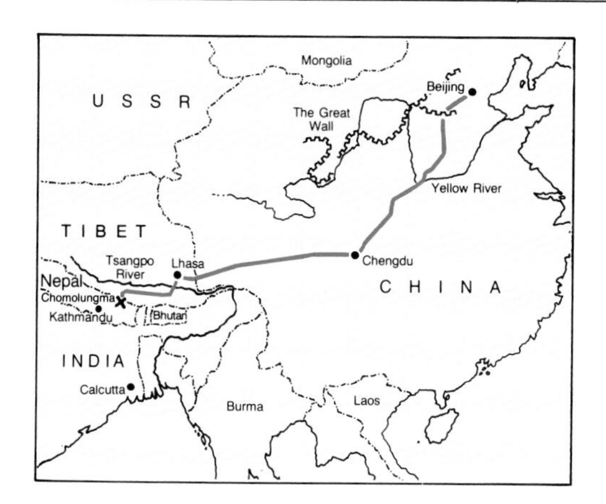

Suddenly Waka called out from the front of the bus, 'There it is!' And indeed there it was, the Mecca of Buddhism — the Potala.

Expedition departures are wretched affairs and the 1985 New Zealand expedition to Chomolungma was no exception. Toyota hosted a lavish farewell party but four hours later, as we prepared to board the plane at Christchurch Airport, tension cut cleanly through the carefully maintained good spirits. As far as our families were concerned we could have been off to war, and the mood was catching. We boarded the plane in that kind of emotional daze which no amount of airline grog will ever touch. Chomolungma '85 was underway. Leader Austin Brookes and deputy leader Bruce Farmer could have been expected to settle down for a couple of hours of pleasant anticipation but soon after take off, the demands of expedition leadership had them busy tidying up a mass of administrative detail.

Their work had started four years before in the aftermath of the highly successful New Zealand Alpine Club expedition to Mt Molamenqing (25,740 feet), about 80 miles west of Chomolungma. The first ascent of a major Himalayan mountain had been achieved and a firm friendship with the Chinese Mountaineering Association established, so it was inevitable that the thoughts of some team members should turn to Chomolungma. That Austin and Bruce should emerge as the proposed expedition leaders was ideal. As leaders of the Molamenqing expedition they had built up a rapport with the Chinese Mountaineering Association, both had a great deal of mountaineering experience and, just as importantly, a notable expertise in man-management.

Back home in Invercargill, Austin and Bruce embarked on their four-year saga of negotiation, fund-raising and logistical planning. First they secured New Zealand Alpine Club backing and official permission from the Chinese

Chengdu, a city of a mere four million inhabitants, enjoys a lifestyle that is considerably more relaxed than the much more populous Beijing.

Mountaineering Association for an attempt on the west ridge of Chomolungma in post-monsoon 1985. Then Alpine Club members in New Zealand and Australia were invited to apply to join the expedition, the remaining twelve members were selected, and at Easter 1982 the first expedition meeting convened.

Top of the agenda was fund-raising. The total cost of the expedition, NZ$165,000, was clearly beyond the personal resources of the members, so a rigorous programme of approaches to potential sponsors, raffles and club-level fund-raising was instituted. As well, the members committed themselves to contributing $5,000 each. A host of companies donated their products and the Ministries of Recreation and Sport and Foreign Affairs gave cash grants totalling $12,500. The New Zealand Alpine Club provided a cash grant from its expedition fund and its members formed the majority of subscribers to our raffle-type fund-raising ventures.

Devaluation in 1984 was to cost us dearly and the search for money to cover our loss continued right into the final days before departure. Happily, Austin and Bruce deftly steered the expedition's finances through this final difficulty and we boarded our plane on 20 July fully solvent.

Our flight to Beijing was the first time the fourteen of us had ever been

Pip Lynch, Ross Cullen and their baby, Ben, at the container packing weekend in Dunedin, February 1985. Pip and Ross masterminded the tedious and complex collection and packing of our food.

Austin Brookes
Age 45. Secondary school deputy principal. Climbed in many parts of the world including the British Isles, Arctic Norway, Swedish Lapland, French Alps, Italian Dolomites, Patagonia, Andes, New Zealand Alps and the Himalaya. Leader 1976 Southland expedition to Cerro Stokes and Mt Aconcagua. Leader 1981 New Zealand Alpine Club expedition to Mt Molamenqing. Notable New Zealand ascents include Sheila Face of Mt Cook (first ascent) and North Face of Mt Haast (first ascent).

Graeme Dingle
Age 39. Writer and businessman. New Zealand ascents include Caroline Face of Mt Cook (second ascent), South Face of Mt Hicks (first ascent), Little North Face of Mt Sabre (first ascent), South Ridge of Mt Cook (first winter ascent), a winter traverse of the Southern Alps. In Europe, the first ascent of the six classic North Faces in one season. Many expeditions to the Andes and Himalaya including first traverse of Yerupaja, Jannu north face and Ocean to the Sky. First traverse of the Himalaya.

Mike Perry
Age 29. Commercial photographer. New Zealand climbs include North Face of Mt Hicks, North Face of Mt Torres (first winter ascent), Caroline and Hooker Faces of Mt Cook. Overseas climbs include ascents of the Nose, Salathe and Zodiac routes on El Capitan in Yosemite Valley, California. (John Ings)

Hugh Van Noorden
Age 26. Primary school teacher. New Zealand ascents include south faces of Mts Douglas, Hicks and Sabre, the Caroline and Sheila Faces of Mt Cook and North Ridge of Mt Sefton (solo). Ascent of Mt Baruntse (23,600 feet).

Shaun Norman
Age 42. Mountain guide and ski instructor. Climbed in British Isles, Austrian Alps and the Pyrenees. Expeditions to the Andes, Mt Erebus (leader) and two ascents of Mt McKinley. New Zealand ascents include South Ridge of Mt Cook and East Face of Mt Walter (winter).

Mike Andrews
Age 38. Lands and Survey parks assistant. Seven first ascents in Tierra del Fuego in 1971. Completed a new route on East Face of Mt Huascaran in 1973. Member 1977 New Zealand Everest expedition. Many new routes in New Zealand including South Face of Mt Haast, and traverse of Malte Brun range. (Dick Price)

Mike Rheinberger
Age 46. Engineering executive. Expeditions include Dharamsura (deputy leader), Changabang (leader), Nanda Devi (leader), Kwangoe and Kanguru.

Rob Blackburne
Age 26. Dentist. Expeditions to Karakorum and Mt Kenya (ice-window route). New Zealand first ascents include South-east Face of Mt Chudleigh and East Face of Mt Burns. (Graeme Dingle)

Warwick Anderson
Age 31. Secondary school teacher. New Zealand climbs include the North Buttress of Mt Sabre (first winter ascent), Caroline, East and Sheila Faces of Mt Cook, Heemskirk Face of Mt Tasman (winter), Spencer Face of Mt Elie de Beaumont (first winter ascent), the North and South Faces of Mt Hicks. Expedition to Mt Molamenqing in 1981.

Dick Price
Age 38. Medical practitioner. New Zealand ascents include Bowie Ridge of Mt Cook, North Ridge of Mt Cook (first winter ascent). Overseas climbing includes British Isles and northern India. Expeditions include 1977 New Zealand expedition to Mt Everest and 1981 New Zealand Alpine Club expedition to Mt Molamenqing.

Peter Allen
Age 32. Urban planner. Expeditions to East Qulu, Mt Changabang and Mt Nilgiri in the Himalaya. Ascent of Mt McKinley in Alaska.

Steve Bruce (left)
Age 25. Police officer. Ascent of Mt Baruntse (23,600 feet). Climbed Mt Cook by nine different routes, including two solo ascents. Traversed western side of the Southern Alps from Preservation Inlet to Nelson, and ascents of the south faces of Mts Douglas and Hicks, the North Buttress of Mt Sabre and the Gledhill Buttress on Mt Nazomi.

Ross Cullen (centre)
Age 37. Economist. New Zealand ascents include South-west Ridge of Mt D'Archiac, South-east Face of Mt Ward, a traverse of Mts Hopkins, Black Tower and McKerrow, and South-east Face of Mt Chudleigh (first ascent). Expedition to the Andes.

Bruce Farmer (right)
Age 38. Metallurgist. New Zealand ascents include Syme-Silberhorn traverse of Mt Tasman, the East Face of Mt La Perouse and the East Ridge of Mt Cook. Member 1976 Southland expedition to Cerro Stokes and Mt Aconcagua. Deputy leader of 1981 New Zealand Alpine Club expedition to Mt Molamenqing. Former President of New Zealand Alpine Club. (Dick Price)

together. The cynics in New Zealand had been outspoken in their criticism of our expedition because of this: they felt we were bound to have an unhappy time because we did not know each other and traditionally, nationally-selected expeditions are loaded with 'prima donnas' determined to achieve their own ends and not prepared to work as a team. Usually these expeditions are emotional nightmares and physical failures. But the cynics had not reckoned on our determination to succeed as a team and on the brilliant leadership of Austin Brookes.

Most of the long flight was spent signing countless postcards which had been pre-sold as a fund-raising exercise. The purchasers had addressed the cards and written a message, usually to a friend. We signed them and would post them from Tibet. Most of the messages said things like, 'Spending my holidays this year on Mt Everest — wish you were here'.

One unusual one said: 'Dear Ian, have got this beaut job as head gardener for the Qomolangma (Mt Everest) Dahlia Society. Would love to get you in the cabbage patch. Love Carol.'

Three others were unsigned political statements:

> To Bob Jones [millionaire property-developer and former New Zealand Party leader]: Dear Bob, land values aren't too great around here although past civilisations have installed very high-rise caves — makes the BNZ bank look smaller than a bread box. Mind you that's all we need to hold NZ's present cash reserves.
>
> To Rt Hon. David Lange [Prime Minister]: Dear Dave, the Americans believe in a nuclear free Pacific. They'll supply all the nuclear weapons we need for free!
>
> To Sir Robert Muldoon [former Prime Minister, with reference to Muldoon's action to remove some handicapped Japanese climbers from Mt Cook and his later attempt to regain leadership]: Dear Rob, hang on in there. No — don't let go! Much love, Japanese Suicide Squad (High Altitude Division).

By the time we flew over Taiwan the signatures of the 'hard core', led by an outrageously drunk and noisy Shaun Norman, had become quite unrecognisable.

Beijing Airport was immaculately clean and tidy. As we claimed our mountain of baggage and made our way through customs we were interested to see Chinese tourists moving smoothly through loaded with TVs, videos, microwave ovens and other electronic trappings of the western world. The age of beep had arrived in China too.

Austin was surprised that there was no representative from the Chinese Mountaineering Association to meet us but on phoning the New Zealand embassy he realised that we were expected the following day. Carl Worker from the embassy came to our rescue with accommodation. In good old friendly Kiwi fashion he quickly arranged billets with the embassy staff, and while Austin phoned, a pretty girl practised her English on the unprotesting Kiwi boys.

We had arrived in Beijing on the hottest night of the year. As we drove through

the streets with the temperature hovering around the mid forties, the Chinese were bringing their beds out on to the pavements. This is a city of extremes — in the winter it can go as low as -20°C.

We enjoyed our few days in Beijing. On the whole the Chinese are very friendly despite the sometimes infuriating way they have of being totally uncooperative. In South America they have the curse of *manana;* in China the equivalent is *mei-yo,* which liberally translated means 'I don't know', 'I don't care', 'go away' or perhaps all three. The socialist system does not assist this: usually there is no incentive for a hotel worker or taxi driver or shop assistant to go out of their way to give service. The taxi system is an infuriating example of this. Despite large numbers of modern imported cabs, it was often impossible to get one because the driver had a dose of the dreaded *mei-yo*s; on several occasions I battled my way into cabs and just sat there until the driver decided it was easier to take me where I wanted to go.

On our first morning in Beijing we met our interpreter 'James', and under his guidance began to tick off the tourist spots of Beijing until our minds were

From the Museum of the Revolution in Beijing one looks out over Tian-an men Square to the Great Hall of the People. The long queue of visitors to Mao's mausoleum (out of photograph to left) is visible just beyond the columns in the foreground. (Steve Bruce)

432

boggled by old national monuments, and James began to understand what a bunch of bloody-minded individualists he had been saddled with for the next two months.

Of course we had to see the patriarch of the revolution, Chairman Mao Zedong, in his crystal tomb and mausoleum in Tian-an men Square. Everyone from China as well as the rest of the world seemed to be there: on open days tens of thousands of people form orderly queues and file respectfully through Mao's mausoleum. Wherever you go in China Mao's eyes seem to stare down at you from paintings and colossal concrete statues. Recently Mao's status has been revised downwards from secular god to 'great man' and it is fashionable to consider the faults of his personality. Of course we were no exception to this rule: as we filed past his body along with thousands of others, Ross Cullen said, 'He's supposed to be among the ten greatest criminals of all time,' and someone else added, 'Jeez ... he's looking a bit yellow around the gills.' I took a nervous look up at the surveillance cameras and moved quickly on.

China loves its children, each one quite probably being mum and dad's one-and-only. With red school ties and after-school smiles this mob's off home.

Recycled leisure — China's dynastic palaces and temples are now public playgrounds. This photograph was taken while strolling through the grounds of the Summer Palace, Beijing.

One morning in a fit of guilt because I hadn't run for two days I left our hotel, the Bei Wei, and loped off towards the Great Hall of the People. It was before 6 am but already the streets were busy with people, mostly on their way to work, but many were just exercising or playing ball games in the street. Outside the Great Hall a line of people were doing Tai Chi and stretching on a railing. Their initial looks of curiosity at my sweating foreign form soon turned to looks of approval as I joined them. Running back towards our hotel I decided that I didn't feel as conspicuous running here in Beijing as I would in a western city.

All around me hundreds of thousands or possibly millions were riding bikes, many of them with side-cars attached containing fat little aristocratic-looking cherubs — products of the one child per couple law. This attempt to bring China's population of a billion-plus under control will undoubtedly have far-reaching effects as that generation comes to power: the infants are obviously their parents' most valuable possession and are treated like royalty. The penalty for having an extra child is a fine of 1000 yuan (NZ$750).

On my run I also couldn't help noting the pleasing forms of the mothers, dressed fashionably, often in tight jeans — a marked contrast to the formless 'Mao suits' worn by both men and women only a few years ago. After getting myself hopelessly lost (bad news in China as hardly anyone speaks English), I finally regained the Bei Wei Hotel in a state of mild exhaustion.

The Beijing heat had turned us into air-conditioning junkies, and our days there were punctuated by sweaty treks from one air-conditioned oasis to the next. Our personal mini-bus became much loved for its cool interior, so too the hotel's reception area. But definitely the biggest island of coolness was the Museum of the Revolution in Tian-an men Square. There, Bruce Farmer noted a rather subtle piece of political persuasion: only the section of the museum concerned with the revolution boasted air-conditioning, the natural history and imperial dynasty sections being positively tropical. No prizes for guessing which part of the museum attracted the masses.

So it was with some dismay that we discovered upon boarding our train in Beijing that it was without air-conditioning. To add to the discomfort each 4-person 6-foot-square compartment had been ingeniously crammed with our luggage in order to avoid the hefty excess baggage charges. However the squalor of our cramped sauna on wheels proved to be the ideal environment for the lowering of barriers and a crucial period of team building.

The train took us south from Beijing to Chengdu, a fascinating forty-hour journey, which would have reduced a steam train enthusiast to a pool of jibbering ecstasy. At every major station and siding the great steaming black monsters hissed a challenge at shiny new electric locos. For two days we sped south-west across plains green with crops of corn where peasants were using farming practices which had scarcely changed for hundreds of years. Many of them lived in houses cut into the cliffs and hillsides beside the railway line.

Ross Cullen refutes the Great Wall's reputation for impregnability. (Graeme Dingle)

Chengdu was hotter than Beijing, the women more beautiful and the Sichuan food infinitely more palatable. This is a comparatively small city — about the same population as New Zealand. Huge hoardings expounded the virtues of the one-child family and so on. One even advertised international goodwill with the words: 'The internationale will be the world'.

At Chengdu Zoo the great cuddly giant pandas were really suffering in the heat. They were slumped against their cage walls like fat Mexicans at siesta time, their tongues hanging out and limbs thrown out wide in a comical 'take me now' pose. I leaned over and scratched one of them behind the ear. His face seemed to contort into a grimace of ecstasy as he tried to force his ear through the bars.

Next day we flew westwards over the mountains of the Chamdo Region towards Lhasa. We darted from one side of the old Boeing 707 to the other, excitedly trying to recognise the high mountains that drifted not that far beneath

---

Beijing Railway Station, temperature about 40°C and a foretaste of the crowded conditions to come on the train. (Mike Andrews)

A farming hamlet on the outskirts of Chengdu. Every few hundred yards there is a hamlet like this, or often a bigger dormitory type of settlement dating from the collective era.

our altitude of 30,000 feet. To the left the huge valley system of the Tsangpo scribed an indefinite line through the mountains. Beyond, somewhere in a shambles of high peaks which were the Eastern Himalaya, was the highest unclimbed mountain in the world, Namche Bawar (25,445 feet). It is a mysterious peak, towering above the Tsangpo gorge, 15,000 to 22,000 feet above it depending on whether the height is taken from the entrance to the gorge or the exit. The mountain is a true eastern corner-post of the Himalaya, as around it the mighty Tsangpo swings in a great horseshoe to plunge nearly 10,000 feet in 100 miles to become the Brahmaputra as it flows into India. After Chomolungma the next dream was to get permission to attempt Namche Bawar and also to jetboat up the Tsangpo.

The airport was in the Tsangpo valley, three hours' drive from Lhasa. In contrast to the thick warm air of Chengdu we stepped out into the thin cool air of nearly 12,000 feet. All around us brown hills rose to rounded summits of more than 18,000 feet that were dusted with new snow. This was the forbidden land of Tibet, closed to westerners until 1980. Until then Tibet had been visited only by the most hardened travellers, such as Marco Polo and Jesuit priests, and in more recent years men like Shipton and Tilman. Tibet had remained a mysterious Buddhist enclave on the 'Roof of the World', ruled by colourful reincarnates called Dalai Lamas. Through the centuries there have been armed conflicts between Nepal, Tibet and China, with Tibet often giving a good account of itself despite the so-called pacifist Buddhist administration.

In 1910 there was a Chinese invasion of Tibet but, following a revolution in 1911, they were ejected and for the next thirty-nine years, up to 1950, the British enjoyed the privilege of being the only official foreign influence. In 1950, only two years after the Maoist revolution in China, the Chinese came marching back, and Tibet embarked on three decades of upheaval and bloodshed.

To begin with the invasion was not a particularly savage one. The fourteenth Dalai Lama, then aged sixteen, initially fled to India but returned to his Potala palace in Lhasa at the request of his people. Life was relatively quiet for a few years but in the mid 1950s the Tibetans began to fight back and in 1959 the Dalai Lama, under threat of imprisonment or death, fled to exile in India. This began twenty years of agony for Tibet as the uprisings were put down ruthlessly and the country was ravaged by the cultural revolution. Ancient monasteries were destroyed, thousands were executed, prisons and concentration camps overflowed and people starved in the countryside. By the mid 1970s the final pockets of resistance had crumbled and in 1980 Tibet opened its doors to the outside world.

New Zealanders were amongst the first to take advantage of the new situation. An expedition led by Austin Brookes climbed Molamenqing, which to this day remains the highest peak climbed by a New Zealand expedition. (The previous highest was Mukut Parbat, 23,760 feet, climbed by Earl Riddiford, Ed Cotter, Ed Hillary and George Lowe in 1951.) Apart from Austin, three other veterans of the Molamenqing expedition were with us: Bruce Farmer, a sometimes frighteningly enthusiastic and prodigiously strong metallurgist from Invercargill, who had been deputy leader on Molamenqing and who assumed this same position on our trip; Dick Price, the energetic climbing doctor, who had looked after everyone's health

so well on Molamenqing and who was to do the same for us; and Warwick Anderson (whom I called Waka), a schoolteacher from Greymouth, who had lost most of his toes to frost-bite on that climb in 1981 and was with us both as a climber and journalist.

As we drove by bus up the valley of the Tsangpo I thought about the effort of the British to determine whether this was the same river as the mighty Brahmaputra. It seemed too incredible that a river could rise in western Tibet, flow 930 miles across the Tibetan plateau and then turn abruptly south to cut through the Himalaya. But all the great rivers of the Indian sub-continent have their major sources to the north of the Himalaya. The Sutlej, Indus, Ganges and Brahmaputra have their headwaters near the sacred mountain called Kailash by the Hindus and Kangrimpoche by the Buddhists, and they all defy the normal laws governing rivers and flow south through the ranges. The Arun, a great tributary of the Ganges, actually flows within half a mile of the Tsangpo at one point near Tingri, before turning south to cut through the Himalaya between Makalu and

Adobe telegraph posts are the most visible legacy of the British presence in Tibet during the early part of this century. Wood was (and still is) scarce but mud plentiful, hence the curious choice of materials. The posts are still in use.

Kanchenjunga, while the Tsangpo continues east for several hundred miles until it cuts through east of Namche Bawar. The reason for this incredible phenomenon is that the rivers were there before the mountains. When the Indian sub-continent, part of the ancient southern continent of Gondwanaland, collided with Asia five million years ago, the Himalaya was pushed up very quickly while the rivers continued to cut down through the soft sedimentary rocks of the new range.

British attempts to prove that the Tsangpo and Brahmaputra were one and the same were unsuccessful until 1913. In that year Major Frederick Bailey with Henry Morshead proved that they were the same river in a particularly daring and dangerous journey, which earned them the disapproval of the Indian government but the gold medal of the Royal Geographic Society.

Perhaps the most amazing attempt to prove that the two rivers were the same was that of a Sikkimese called Kinthup, who in August 1880 trekked into Tibet disguised as the servant of a Mongolian lama. Kinthup's brief was to place 500 logs with a special marking in the Tsangpo at a predetermined time, when observers would be watching the Brahmaputra in Assam. Unfortunately poor Kinthup was sold into slavery by his lama in exchange for a horse. Undiscouraged he escaped and sent a message to India telling of his misfortunes and rearranging the date on which the logs would be put into the Tsangpo. He then cut the logs, placed fifty per day into the Tsangpo for ten days, and then trekked back to India. The entire gambit had taken over four years, but Kinthup appears to have been a particularly unfortunate character. The message he had sent had never reached India and the 500 logs had passed into the Bay of Bengal unnoticed.

As we travelled in comfort up the valley of the Tsangpo I also looked out at the river and appraised its jetboating possibilities. It looked good but I had no doubt that unseen gorges would add some excitement to such an expedition. After an hour's travelling we stopped to photograph a huge stone image of Buddha carved into a cliff, then shortly afterwards we crossed a long concrete bridge across the Tsangpo, guarded at each end by Chinese soldiers.

The road now continued up the attractive Kyi valley towards Lhasa. The fields were green with new barley and the rustic stone houses clung together for support. To begin with there did not seem to be many people about but the further we went, the more crowded the road became. Yaks and donkey carts competed for space with Tibetans on foot, as well as buses, Chinese trucks and jeeps.

Then the valley opened out and suddenly Waka called out from the front of the bus, 'There it is!' And indeed there it was, the Mecca of Buddhism — the Potala, said to be able to accommodate 10,000 monks. The monastery is built atop a small hill overlooking the city, its golden roof gleaming in the midday sun, and to the awestruck onlooker it has the appearance of a mountain and a monastery rolled into one.

The Potala, formerly the winter palace of the Dalai Lama, is said to contain 1,000 rooms and is recognised the world over as the symbol of Tibetan Buddhism and culture. Miraculously spared the depredatory attention of the Red Guard during the cultural revolution but now largely bereft of monks, the Potala seems destined to be a Tibetan tourist attraction.

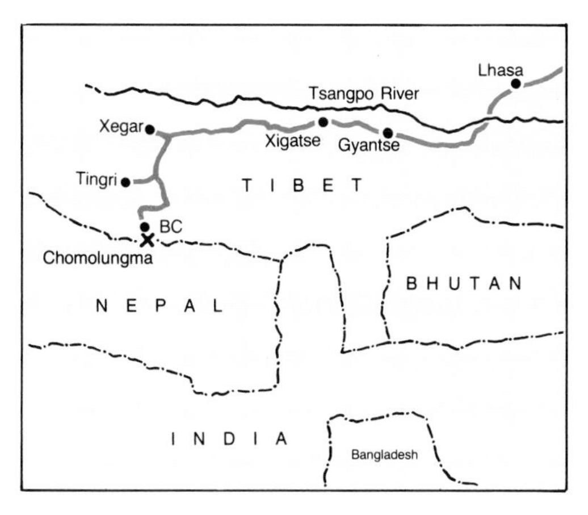

It looked much steeper than I had imagined and I felt a sudden chill excitement at the anticipation of climbing it.

We were billeted 2 miles from the Potala in one of the compounds reserved for foreign visitors, a pleasant little grassy oasis run by friendly Tibetans. Despite the relatively spartan conditions, the Chinese charge a premium for accommodation in these enclaves. But although this is hard on climbers, who are traditionally poor, the basic policy is probably a sound one — to minimise the impact on the Tibetans and the countryside while maximising the profit — and perhaps a lesson for New Zealand.

In the evening Bruce Farmer, Mike Andrews and I threaded our way through the maze of alleys and archways that was old Lhasa. Eventually we emerged into the marketplace, a typical jostling Asian bazaar where organised chaos reigned supreme. Colourful stalls lined the street in haphazard fashion, displaying wares ranging from the basic essentials such as barley and clothes to leopard skins and lockets containing pictures of the Dalai Lama (most Tibetans would probably think of the latter as an essential too).

Jungly Tibetan vendors in traditional heavy clothing plied us with all kinds of rustic junk. Bruce showed some interest in various bits of jewellery, so for a few hundred yards we were dogged by some particularly keen characters who looked as if they had just come from breaking in yaks. Their long hair was done in pigtails, a piece of turquoise hung from their left ear lobes, to prevent them from being reincarnated as a donkey, and from inside their generous barkoos (Tibetan coats) they seemed to be able to produce any trinket, butterlamp, locket or string of semi-precious stones. The socialist revolution had done nothing to blunt the age-old trading skills of these people.

Prayer flags, the ubiquitous symbol of Buddhism, atop a pass. Tibetans believe passes are the home of dangerous spirits and leave these flags as protection.

Our second day in Lhasa was spent exploring the Potala. The guide was a charming and open lady with a cute little freckled nose, called Jang Jiang June. Unlike most of the Chinese that we met she was happy to speak openly on just about any subject.

To reach the Potala we climbed the great line of worn stone steps, feeling a bit like flies on an elephant's backside — the immense monastery with its white stone and ochre walls capped with tarnished gold roof towering 300 feet above us was like a small Chomolungma. The Potala was built on the ruins of an ancient royal palace by perhaps the greatest of the Dalai Lamas, Ngawang Lozang Gyatsu, the Great Fifth, who appears to have united Tibet under the religious philosophy of his Yellow Sect. His teacher was the abbot of Tashilungpo monastery at Xigatse and to him the Great Fifth gave the title of Panchen Rimpoche, Precious Great Scholar. To the Panchen Lamas, who have succeeded each other by a similar process of reincarnation to the Dalai Lamas, fell much of the responsibility for the administration of Tibet. The Mongol chief, Gushri Khan, took responsibility for the defence of the country.

More than 300 years later as I climbed the great stone staircase in front of the Potala I was surprised by my own emotional detachment. I had expected to be overwhelmed by the place. After so many years of wandering through the Himalayan region south of the border, dreaming of a visit to this forbidden shrine, here I was. But somehow my heart was empty. Like so many grand old buildings whose time is gone, the Potala was now a lifeless giant, a reminder of a religious regime that many would sooner forget, a museum of Buddhist bric-à-brac where tourists wheeze up endless staircases, sometimes incongruously equipped with oxygen apparatus!

At the top of the great stone stairway we entered a huge courtyard through an ornate and colourful gateway. Rising several storeys in front of us was the heart of the Potala. Another stairway led into its gloomy recesses where there were enormous bronze and gold effigies of Buddha in his various incarnations. One sensed the priceless value of these things rather than saw it, as the only light came from flickering lamps fuelled by huge quantities of yak butter. The air was thick with its slightly rancid odour mixed with incense and the smell of old wealth and power. Another room contained huge chortens entombing the remains of the thirteen previous Dalai Lamas, with the Great Fifth taking pride of place. They were all plated with pure gold and inlaid with jewels. It is said that the plating on the fifth Dalai Lama's chorten weighs 179,703 ounces.

Dalai Lama means 'Master Ocean of Wisdom' and the first Dalai Lama was Gedun Truppa who founded Tashilungpo monastery at Xigatse in 1447. As we filed past the chortens I wondered whether the fourteenth Dalai Lama would ever return from his exile in India, even if only as a corpse, to be incarcerated beside his predecessors. The Chinese have made no secret that they would like him to

---

Dusk at the door of the Jokang, Tibetan Buddhism's most important place of worship. After years of repression, the faithful can once again pray their way into this deeply religious place in the city of Lhasa.

---

return before this, to take up the reins of all administration apart from the military, but when I spoke with him in 1981 he said with a laugh, 'No way can we go backwards and no use .... but I think I will return there some time'. From this I understood that he did not believe he could return to Tibet to administrate again, but that for personal and philosophical reasons he would like to return for a visit. An Indo-Tibetan friend of mind, Chewang Tashi, told me that the scriptures prophesied he was the last Dalai Lama, but he added shrewdly, 'If there is another he will be a warrior!'

We climbed up more stairs to the roof where we began haggling with the doormen on the Dalai Lama's old suite for a cheaper entry than the normal 2 yuan for foreigners. Like most New Zealanders we were not keen on being ripped off. The Chinese administration was already fleecing us blind to be in Tibet and we were keen to fight back where we could; while Jang Jiang June negotiated for us, we gazed out over the rooftops of Lhasa as if we couldn't care less about a visit to the royal suite. Finally the price was set at 20 fen each, a one thousand percent reduction! 'Bloody tight-fisted New Zealanders' I mumbled, putting the doormen's expressions into words as we filed past.

Inside the suite all was apparently as his excellency had left it. The clock was even stopped at the fateful hour of 11.20 and the calendar recorded the day, although I don't remember what it said. It was a colourful, airy, light and comfortable cell (as lamas' cells go), commanding a fabulous view over the city, but, despite this, one got the feeling of imprisonment: I have no doubt that the sad events that befell Tibet were for the Dalai Lama a release from an inevitable up-market imprisonment. Through his exile, moreover, he has become a worldly and astute politician. As we descended the great stairway Jang Jiang June told us that during the so-called 'cultural revolution' the Red Guard would have destroyed the Potala, but the locals blockaded the palace and eventually the Chinese Army removed the attackers. Many of Tibet's other great monasteries were not so lucky.

In Lhasa we picked up the two vehicles which were to carry us to the foot of Chomolungma. One was a shiny new Toyota Landcruiser, generously donated by the manufacturers and driven by a grinning demon called Mr Chan, whom our dentist, Rob Blackburne, diagnosed on first meeting as having pyorrhoea. The other vehicle was a Chinese copy of a 1936 Chevrolet truck. On to this was loaded our equipment — the Chinese could not believe how little we had. Apparently the 1983 French attempt on the west ridge had had fourteen trucks! (When Rob Blackburne's mother heard of our cheap and light approach she said, 'I've heard on the radio how you're going to do it on a shoestring — can't even afford proper oxygen. You'll come back and have to live as a social security beneficiary!')

One day at lunch we met a breezy Australian woman called Sorrel Wilby who was planning to walk across Tibet with only a yak for company. The authorities finally convinced her that yaks were difficult beasts to look after and a donkey would be more appropriate. To fill in time before her departure to western Tibet she decided to accompany us to base camp. We were delighted to have her feminine company for a few days; we were going to have quite enough of

our own before we were finished.

On the last day of July we left Lhasa and our small convoy was soon climbing away from the Tsangpo valley, grinding laboriously up to the first of many high passes. From the top, at 17,000 feet, we all poured from the bus for a leak and our first good look at the Tibetan countryside. We were atop a gentle but barren ridge. The pass was marked by an enormous heap of stones where a thicket of tattered prayer flags fluttered in the breeze. I added my own to the heap, shouting as I did a Sherpa prayer for safe passage, 'So so so ... la lago oh'. Behind us stretched the hazy valley of the Tsangpo, its braided waters drawing twisted blue fingers across the broad grey bed of shingle. Ahead in our direction of travel lay a large blue lake cradled in an almost green tussock basin, and beyond, the first of the high mountains rose in a sweep of white snow and ice to 21,500 feet. Mike Perry and Waka were setting a fearful pace shooting pictures — I could almost hear the Kodak shares going up.

We stopped for lunch at the far end of the lake in what appeared to be a particularly deserted part of the world. But scarcely had our backsides hit the rocky ground when an enthusiastic crowd of Tibetans were clambering around, jostling

A generation of imposed socialist secularism lies between this middle-aged monk and his junior confrère. Tashilungpo monastery, Xigatse.

each other for the choicest bits of rubbish. Cans and bottles were of particular value. Hugh Van Noorden felt that they were really degrading themselves by scrapping over our castoffs and said so, as only Hugh could. It is not difficult to feel grumpy when you first arrive at high altitude and Shaun told Hugh not to get 'so uptight'. This was the nearest we'd come to a confrontation and the rest of us held our breaths, but fortunately nothing eventuated.

Our next stop of interest was the local petrol station, more like Fort Knox than a petrol station. The fuel was stored within thick walls capped by tangles of barbed wire, and to obtain service we knocked on a small hatch and a creaking little door opened to reveal a suspicious-looking attendant who pushed a nozzle at us through close bars — obviously petrol is a valuable commodity in a land where the yak is still king.

From the lake the road climbed to another high pass. Here glaciers came almost down to the road like giant shattered white staircases from the surrounding peaks. An hour later we were 4,000 feet lower down, driving past fertile fields

Tibetan buildings on the outskirts of Xigatse. A small cluster of drying yak dung can be seen on the centre wall.

Monks in the alleyways of Tashilungpo monastery. Tashilungpo is a joy to visit because it is a living monastery where monks and nuns still practise their religion with all its strange sounds and smells and rituals. (Mike Andrews)

Gold as a roofing material — a status symbol that would be hard to beat. This photo shows a detail of the Tashilungpo monastery.

as we approached Xigatse, second largest town in Tibet. On the western edge of the town was Tashilungpo Gompa, monastery of the Panchen Lama who since the Dalai Lama's exile has been the paramount religious figure in Tibet.

At the time of the 1950 invasion the Panchen Lama was only a young boy and the Chinese were able to use him as a link with the Tibetan people, but as the years went by and conditions deteriorated in his homeland he became more and more outspoken. In the early 1960s he became openly rebellious and in 1964 he was imprisoned in China's main political prison, the dreaded Qin Cheng near Beijing. Conditions were desperate and on one occasion he tried to commit suicide while being tortured. In February 1978, after fourteen years' imprisonment, he was finally released.

Tashilungpo was a joy to visit because it was a living monastery where nuns and lamas, as well as many other ordinary folk, lived and practised their religion. In the monastery's dark, secret recesses monks chanted prayers, banged drums and cymbals and made exceptionally rude noises on horns in an atmosphere thick with incense smoke. Little trees flourished in wonky-paved courtyards and Tibetans with smiling, lined faces poked their heads out of ornate windows where marigolds bloomed in window boxes. Teams of builders worked at renovating the shaky parts of the building, and artists followed behind decorating walls, pillars and ceilings with ornate and colourful designs. Here Buddhism was alive and well.

Next day we headed for Xegar traversing more typically Tibetan countryside, absolutely barren hills rising brown and dry above the green patchwork carpet of barley on the valley floors, with a couple of high passes thrown in for good measure. On top of one of these, at about 17,000 feet, we found fossilised seashells, reminding us that this plateau and the Himalayan range were both once beneath the sea. From a geological point of view this was in the relatively recent past — only five million years ago the Sea of Tethys lapped against the shores of Asia (now southern Tibet). But Gondwanaland crept up in the dark geological night and collided with the ancient shore of Asia: the harder granites, gneisses and basalts of Gondwanaland bit into the soft sedimentary rock of Asia and forced it upward, twisting and wrenching it into the highest and yet youngest of the world's great mountain ranges. Of course the great rivers which were already there cut into the land as it was forced up, creating the incredible gorges that are now the delight of trekkers and the despair of roading engineers. Tibet was then probably clothed in wonderful forests but ultimately the Himalaya became a natural barrier to stop the monsoon rains and the forests died out. Local folklore describes it differently but, like our own Maori legends, contains an uncanny ring of truth.

The legend goes that the almighty Hindu god, Vishnu, lived on the shores of the great Sea. His only companions were a pair of seagulls whose eggs were always being washed away by the waves. Eventually they cried out to Vishnu to help and Vishnu's violent response was to swallow the sea leaving in its place Mother Earth. Exhausted after his work and the inevitable bout of drinking that

Xegar township, and on the ridge above, Xegar Dzong.

followed, Vishnu slept and while he did, a demon called Hiranyanksha violently raped Mother Earth, raped her with such brutality that her limbs were broken and contorted, thus forming the Himalaya.

In the evening we arrived at Xegar, familiar to us through our readings of the early British Everest expeditions and their descriptions of the great fortress on the hillside. We could clearly make out the impressive walls but even from a great distance we could see that the cultural revolution had reduced the once proud dzong (fortress) to little more than a ruin, quite a contrast to one writer's description of the 'White Glass Fort'. It was, however, still a remarkable series of buildings which staggered up a steep hillside like some medieval castle designed by Walt Disney or Ludwig of Bavaria.

We were billeted in an even more basic foreign compound than the one in Lhasa, evidence that we were reaching one of the furthest outposts of tourism. However, this did not affect the cost. In the morning I climbed up towards the old dzong with Bruce Farmer. As we went we held a rather incongruous discussion about the sad state of the New Zealand Alpine Club, a situation that some felt might

Xegar Dzong, a scene of tragic destruction. The cultural revolution reduced almost everything within the walls of Xegar Dzong to rubble — the remains poke skywards like the bones of a giant skeleton picked clean by vultures. (Ross Cullen)

be changed if we were successful on Chomolungma.

On the hillside above us, in the perfectly haphazard way of Tibetan villages, clung the local quarter, a cluster of houses leaning at crazy angles against and on top of each other and possessing a hundred times the character of the orderly Chinese quarter that we had just passed. Above the flat roofs heaped with winter feed for the animals, and the fluttering prayer flags, rose a path cutting diagonally across the steep hillside towards the once proud Xegar Dzong. We met Hugh on the path and together walked up through a narrow gate into a massive walled area. Hugh said seriously, 'I wonder how many people have lost their heads trying to get through here.' Inside was a scene of tragic destruction. The cultural revolution had reduced almost everything within the walls to rubble; the remains poked skywards like a giant skeleton picked clean by vultures. But beyond a low ridge strewn with the remains of once sturdy buildings, a sight totally at odds with the desecration brought tears to my eyes. A group of Tibetans, both men and women, were happily rebuilding the heart of the dzong, the Gompa. The women sang as they shovelled soil through a screen, and the men carried rocks to the new building where carpenters and stonemasons were busy adding the finishing touches to the red and black structure.

Now joined by Rob Blackburne, Peter Allen and Mike Andrews we climbed on up steeper and steeper ground for a few hundred feet to a head wall. One hundred feet above, the fortifications came to an apex on a steep little peak. Every alternative route to this point looked decidedly loose and dangerous and we wondered what form of ladder had taken people there when the place was intact: to us mountaineers it was an irresistible challenge. Hugh disappeared upwards somewhere, Mike and Bruce climbed into a corner where two walls came together and I encouraged Peter and Rob into a kind of vertical chimney with a terrifying drop below. We climbed the chimney, then a difficult little step of about 10 feet had me grunting, and on reaching a ledge I looked down to find Peter and Rob had been frightened off by my efforts and were nowhere to be seen. The next 30 feet were horrible but I was past the point of no return and was thankful to struggle on to the summit to be greeted by a grinning Hugh, 'That's probably the hardest climbing you'll do on the expedition.'

'Yeah, I hope so,' I panted. We walked down the easy back way, stopping at the Gompa long enough to build a small cairn and put some money into it as a contribution to the new building.

In the afternoon we drove towards Tingri, the last stop before base camp. The bus we had been travelling in went no further than Xegar, so we huddled uncomfortably in the back of the truck surrounded by bags of equipment and food. The dusty road drew a stark line across the plain of Tingri and the wild atmosphere was magnified by black monsoon clouds mushrooming all around, growing from the desolate craggy mountains dusted with snow. The mountains were as dark as night in places and brightly lit in others where shafts of sunlight beamed through holes in the cloud.

The old truck droned on throwing up a dust storm behind, covering us with a thick blanket of grey. Sorrel was crammed in happily amongst the boys, a Peruvian

Xegar Dzong. Beyond a low ridge strewn with the remains of once sturdy buildings, a sight totally at odds with the desecration of the dzong brought tears to my eyes. A group of Tibetans, both men and women, were happily rebuilding the heart of the dzong, the Gompa. (Graeme Dingle)

A young woman labourer at Xegar Dzong. (Rob Blackburne)

hat on her head, the grey dust hanging heavily on her eyelashes. Near Tingri the valley suddenly opened out into a kind of high basin surrounded on two sides by the giants of the Himalaya, which glowed in the late afternoon sun like a scene dreamed up by Tolkien.

Tingri was another one of those famous spots that the old British expeditions used as a main camp. It is not surprising; the hot springs there must have felt like paradise to those men so far from the baths of England. The first expedition in 1921 even established base camp there, still about 40 miles from Chomolungma. They would turn in their graves if they knew of the underground missile tracking installations which are rumoured to be in the area now. But they were well concealed and we saw no sign of them.

After a dreadful meal of congealed macaroni cheese, Dick Price, Mike Andrews and I retreated to the luxury of the hot pools. As we lay back letting the hot water gently wash away the dust, we talked of other expeditions and giggled like schoolboys as the hot water caressed our bodies. Overhead, prayer flags fluttered, clouds scudded across the pale moon and the black sky flashed with intermittent lightning. Life seemed pretty good.

It had been decided to spend an extra day at Tingri acclimatising, as one of the problems with approaching the Himalaya from the north is that you gain altitude very quickly. It would have been possible for us to reach base camp from the lowlands in two or three days and one is tempted to hurry because of the high cost of accommodation, but Austin had wisely decided that we should take it quietly. The reason that the early British expeditions were able to make such quick initial progress on the mountain was that they were very fit from the long walk in through Sikkim and westward across Tibet. Walking for weeks at an average altitude of 12-13,000 feet with occasional flurries up to 18,000 feet would be excellent acclimatisation, whereas the modern climber going to base camp after only a few days at high altitude inevitably feels seedy for a week or so. For the first time I was using a new drug called Diamox to assist acclimatisation and although Dick was cynical about its value it was so far proving excellent, and I hadn't had any of the headaches which I would normally have had when first going to a high altitude.

We spent part of the morning discussing tactics for the mountain. This was the first time that Austin had had a chance to show his cards, but in fact he spoke less than the rest. Instead he wisely sounded the team out on their own ideas so that he could develop a plan that would suit the individual temperaments. It was not that he did not have a plan, quite the reverse, but he was playing it cool, waiting until the time was right to show his hand. The old perennial problem about using artificial oxygen or not came up: some wanted to use it if it meant the difference between getting up or not, but most wanted to keep it in reserve and if oxygen-less attempts failed or if we were worn out then we would resort to using it. Bruce was very vocal and super-optimistic: 'If those old guys could get to 28,000 feet

A part of Xegar township showing the typical Tibetan cluster of courtyards and flat-roofed mud houses. Even at 14,000 feet the barley fields beyond the houses are lush. (Ross Cullen)

in tweed suits, then we should be able to do it easily with all our fancy plastic stuff.' The rest of the day was devoted to kite flying and preparing for the trip to base camp.

Mike Rheinberger and I drew the long straws for travel on 5 August. We rode comfortably in the back of the new Toyota although at times it was not altogether clear that we had got the best part of the bargain. We were crammed in the back, our legs arranged carefully around tins and bags with our heads uncomfortably near the roof. Whenever Mr Chan hit a bump or pot hole we would be bounced upwards, striking our heads on the roof. Chan drove in the laid-back manner of most Chinese who have learned to drive in the army. To our horror and displeasure he did not slow down for many things: heavy roading machinery would cause him reluctantly to reduce pressure on the accelerator, but people, animals, bumps and craters would be dispatched in a cloud of flying stones and dust. He only changed gears when the protesting engine could not handle the strain any longer. Perhaps his two least endearing habits were going round blind corners on the wrong side and tearing down hill in Chinese overdrive, only braking for hairpin bends at the very last moment. Toyota Landcruiser was made for this man, or at least he thought so. Sitting beside Chan was our liaison officer, Wang Song-ping or 'Pine Tree' as he asked us to call him. He was a withdrawn, handsome man, sporting a shock of straight dark hair and academic-looking glasses.

The road to Chomolungma branched abruptly off the main Tingri-Xegar highway and headed north. Suddenly the road was reduced to little more than bumpy ruts and it was not long before Rheinberger wished he had worn his crash hat rather than his flat cap. We passed through a typically rustic and simple Tibetan village surrounded by small fields, each family's plot carefully divided from others by rough stone walls. In the fields people in heavy dark clothing went about their work, aware only of the need to produce food before the winter made growing impossible and life itself would be a struggle.

As we began zigzagging up towards the pass we marvelled at the road engineering. On the uphill side the road had been cut out of the mountain, on the downhill side it had been built up with rock. This was the remarkable road built by that first Chinese expedition to Chomolungma in 1960. The crest of the pass was about 18,000 feet (probably the highest road in the world) and as we reached it we were suddenly treated to the most dramatic view of the Himalaya that either of us had ever seen. Even though still 24 miles away the sight of Chomolungma took our breath away, towering head and shoulders above the rest, a gigantic white pyramid. It looked much steeper than I had ever imagined and I felt a sudden chill excitement at the anticipation of climbing it.

'That must be the Kang Chung face,' said Mike in awe.

'Yeah ... I can see the Hillary Step on the summit ridge,' I added, heaping

---

Cho Oyu from near the town of Tingri.

Chomolungma and, in the foreground Tingri hot springs. At Tingri we acclimatised for a few days before moving up to base camp. At first, the area seemed quite deserted but early on our first evening there we noticed a Tibetan watching impassively from just beyond our tents. Next morning we discovered that the barren landscape boasted a couple of villages and a number of seasonal encampments. (Hugh Van Noorden)

Beneath prayer flags and haze from burning yak dung, the day begins in a Tibetan village.

Peasant women near Gyantse drying grain. The Tibetan harvest is a medieval affair, a long cycle of human drudgery that concedes little to mechanisation.

Dawn near the Kathmandu-Lhasa highway.

mistake on mistake (this was to cost me dearly later when I saw Mike Perry again). To the east of Chomolungma stood the massive bulk of Cho Oyu and Gyang Kang Chung, to the west was graceful Makalu. Our Chinese friends were apparently unmoved as Rheinberger and I danced about clicking off pictures sixty to the dozen.

The descent from the pass was another bumpy head-whacking nightmare. In places the old weathered mud walls of houses long gone stood as a sad reminder that people had not respected the delicate balance in this high country where overgrazing can cause almost irreversible problems. In another place an ancient fortified ruin on an unapproachable-looking crag indicated the warlike past when clans conquered and plundered each other at will.

Down on the banks of the river in the broad Rongbuk valley we passed through the first of a number of villages that were untouched by time apart from the road, and that appeared to have had little influence. Some little kids in ragged clothes and bare feet chased the jeep or hid shyly behind walls, but their parents showed little reaction to our passing.

The rubble which was Rongbuk monastery. (Ross Cullen)

A craftswoman repainting frescoes at Rongbuk monastery. During the cultural revolution the Red Guard systematically destroyed Rongbuk monastery, which at 16,500 feet is thought to be the highest monastery in the world. Now, a dedicated group of eight monks and nuns is restoring the monastery at a rate of about one room each year. The monastery has several hundred rooms.

After several miles our track disappeared into the milky waters of the Rongbuk river. It looked like a desperate crossing for a small jeep so I took my trousers off and with some difficulty waded across to test the depth. The water was so cold it hurt my legs and by the time I had tried several different places to find the best crossing my teeth were chattering so badly they were in danger of shattering against each other and my jaw muscles were sore. We were beginning to wonder if we might have to wait until the nightly freeze reduced the flow but Chan was made of sterner stuff. With more luck than skill he ploughed the brave little Toyota into the soupy torrent, stalled the engine, then decided to put it into low ratio with a graunch that made our blood run cold, and just when we thought the Toyota was about to be tested as a submarine the wheels clawed their way across the boulders and up the far bank. But for good Sino-New Zealand relationships, Chan could have found himself in a more passive role in the back seat.

At about 2 pm we passed the ruins of the once proud Rongbuk monastery at 16,500 feet. This ancient holy place had once housed dozens of monks who welcomed many expeditions; indeed most of the expeditions up to 1948 set up their base camp here. Like Xegar Dzong, Rongbuk had been destroyed and along with it many of the monks, but like Xegar it was currently enjoying a revival, several monks and nuns living here again. They had much work to do.

Three miles beyond Rongbuk we rolled into base camp and tumbled, punch-drunk and whoozy from the high altitude, out of the Toyota. Rheinberger took off his flat cap to show three nasty wounds where his head had struck the Toyota's roof.

Base camp was a tiny green flat at the base of a moraine where a little spring spilled into a rather septic-looking pool. Scattered around this rubbish-cluttered pool were the tents of a large Catalonian expedition and a small French one. A skinny and lame dog seemed to epitomise the place as it dragged a bit of dirty offal around. As we approached the main tent Rheinberger advised me, 'Don't call them Spanish, they are very sensitive about it'. We had nothing to worry about, however, as only the Chinese liaison people and the cook were there; everyone else was on the hill.

We were welcomed with a bowl of tasty noodles and then we asked the crucial question, 'Could we camp here?' The request was not treated with great enthusiasm but the liaison officer agreed to ask the Catalan leader by radio. The answer came back, a positive 'No'.

'They've got a bloody cheek to think that they have some kind of exclusive right,' I moaned.

'Yeah, but it's not a very nice place anyway. Let's go and look at the one further up the valley,' said Rheinberger with his usual good sense.

Six hundred yards further on just below the snout of the Rongbuk glacier was a barren little flat beneath a small hill of debris. On top of the hill were memorials to most of the people who had died on the north side of Chomolungma

---

From the summit of the pass before the Rongbuk valley we were greeted with a broad vista dominated by Chomolungma. To the east sat this giant wedge, Makalu (27,790 feet).

since 1980, among them the American woman, Marty Hoey, who had fallen down the Great Gully in 1983, and Peter Boardman and Joe Tasker, the two brilliant English climbers who had disappeared on the north-east route. A pretty depressing place to have a camp we agreed, but we did not have much choice.

Once the rest of the team arrived in the old truck they concurred that this was the place, so ignoring headaches and lethargy we got stuck into the job of levelling tent sites, pitching tents and cleaning up the Chinese, American, British and Japanese rubbish that was spread liberally about. Sorrel made copious brews and during one of our regular stops we vigorously discussed the view that we had seen from the top of the pass. I foolishly said what a fabulous view it had been of the Kang Chung face. 'That wasn't the Kang Chung face,' challenged Mike Perry. So sure was I, that I laid a $50 wager on it. I was later proved wrong and Mike was $50 richer.

On 8 August with base camp pitched, the old truck returned to Lhasa taking with it Sorrel. We were all a little sad to see her go and shouted our good wishes to her and her donkey-to-be as the truck rattled away across the grey Rongbuk stones.

Mike Perry describes the truck passengers' reactions to base camp: 'At the end of a long day's jolting in the back of our truck, the best option for a base camp site appalled us. At best, the shingle pit that was our chosen site was bleak.'

The team, resplendent in Levis, at base camp and in the background, Chomolungma. Standing, left to right: Ross Cullen, Graeme Dingle, Shaun Norman, Bruce Farmer, Rob Blackburne, Mike Andrews, Dick Price, Warwick Anderson, Peter Allen and Steve Bruce. Crouching, left to right: Mike Perry, Hugh Van Noorden, Michael Rheinberger and Austin Brookes. Insets: left, Pine Tree (Dick Price) *and right, James Wu.*

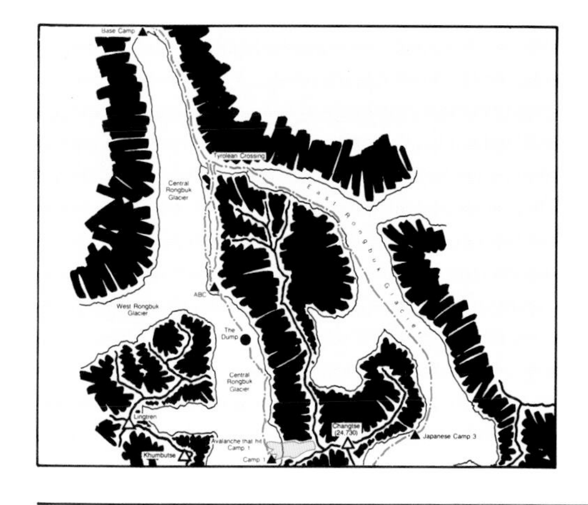

The steep and narrow Hornbein Couloir was the focus of our concentration, it was certainly the crux of the west ridge route.

The west ridge of Chomolungma was the first of the 'harder' routes to be climbed. In 1963, ten years after Chomolungma was first climbed, a strong American team set about making the third ascent.* There were two 'pushers' on this trip who were not satisfied simply to re-climb the south-east ridge. Tom Hornbein and Willi Unsoeld with minimal support from the rest of the team pulled off one of the greatest achievements in the history of Himalayan climbing by ascending the west ridge and traversing the mountain down the south-east ridge, thus turning just another ascent of Chomolungma into an extraordinary feat of mountaineering. Hornbein and Unsoeld avoided the difficulties of the west ridge crest by climbing a deep gully on the north face now called the Hornbein Couloir. Since that fabulous success of 1963 the actual ridge had been climbed by both Yugoslavs and Bulgarians. All of these ascents had been made from Nepal, as had two notable failures involving New Zealanders.

In the post-monsoon season of 1981 two New Zealanders, Russell Bryce and Paddy Freaney, took up a lapsed commission and launched a spirited two-man attempt on the Hornbein/Unsoeld route. They reached the foot of the Hornbein Couloir but the weather forced them back. Three years later, Peter Hillary set out to lead an Australasian group up the same route. From their top camp near the

*The Swiss had made the second ascent in 1956. They also made the first ascent of Lhotse during this same expedition.

Peter Allen on our Tyrolean crossing of the East Rongbuk stream. The instability of the anchors and uncertain origins of the rope became the subject of much black humour. However, the rope's most memorable moment came when it was blatantly stolen by descending yak-herders. (Shaun Norman)

foot of the Hornbein, Kim Logan, Fred From, John Muir, Peter Hillary and Craig Nottle set off for the top at 2.30 am. Strengthening wind caused Muir, Hillary and Nottle to turn back but at 7.30 am as they approached the camp Nottle fell 1,400 feet to his death from a relatively straight-forward crampon slope. At that time From and Logan were climbing a step at about 26,800 feet. When they saw Nottle fall they too descended, but as they reached the same spot Fred From also fell to his death down the Couloir. It was a tragic end to a bold attempt.

By August 1985, as we stood in base camp looking up at the north face of Chomolungma, the west ridge had still never been climbed from Tibet despite attempts by strong American and French teams. All too aware of the growing list of New Zealand failures in the Himalaya we dearly wanted success, but most of us were not prepared to achieve it at the cost of lives.

From base camp, Chomolungma was impressive, even though she was still 12 miles away. Sixty-four years ago Mallory had also been impressed from this angle, 'I wish some folk could see the precipice from this site — a grim spectacle most unlike the long gentle slope suggested by photos ... E. is a rock mountain.'

The vast bulk of Chomolungma, still 6 miles away from here at advance base camp, seemed the size of three ordinary mountains stacked up, one on top of the other. The west ridge rises directly above the figures, follows the long flat skyline and climbs steeply for the last 4,000 feet to the summit.

That was pre-monsoon 1921. In post-monsoon 1985 Chomolungma was far from that: she rose a brilliant white pyramid, filling the head of the Rongbuk. To the right of the summit pyramid, the steep west spur ascended to a relatively flat section of the west ridge at about 24,000 feet. Then there was just over half a mile of gently undulating snow arete to around 25,000 feet. At that point the rocky west ridge swept upwards for nearly 4,000 feet in a series of steep steps. To its left the deep white scar of the Hornbein snaked up towards the top. This was the way we intended to go. Further to the left of the Hornbein, the Great Gully cut a swathe up the centre of the north face. The left-hand or north ridge looked easy but it held problems of its own as the Catalans were finding out at that moment.

Peter Allen had brought with him a powerful telescope through which on 8 August we watched two Catalans and two Nepalis making very slow progress upwards from their camp at about 26,800 feet.

This was the second Catalan attempt on Chomolungma. In 1983 they had come in the post-monsoon season like us, but had been forced back from high on the mountain by the gales that begin to blow during early October. This time,

Dick Price carries the 'field hospital' through the wasteland between base camp and advance base camp. Dick's vast medical kit at base camp held medical science's answers to a depressingly broad range of potential ailments. (Steve Bruce)

Alpine Guides

trusting in Messner's theory that there was a better chance of success during the monsoon, they had mounted their attempt during July and August. Now they were discovering that there were problems of another kind — deep soft snow. We could see them ploughing a furrow slowly up to a position for camp six at about 27,500 feet.

Diary: 10 August. Last night there was a violent rainstorm. In the evening Doctor Dick did his house calls — took blood pressures (mine is 120 over 84 which is pretty good considering). He checked for retinal haemorrhages, which would indicate bad acclimatisation. Rob had several, but it doesn't seem to have slowed him down. After Dick had left, the storm began in earnest — the tents were shaken by gusts of wind and very heavy rain lashed down. Would you believe it, my bowels chose this time to be stricken by the first dose of diarrhoea. I ran from the tent but sadly didn't make the loo. I took my clothes off, buried them under a cairn of rocks and fled naked, wet and freezing, back to the tent. I wonder how the Catalans have fared?

Breakfast was a hilarious affair as everyone exchanged tales of the night's adventures — Rheinberger seemed to delight in bodily function stories more than most. Everyone laughed heartily as he described his first-ever experience of using a pee bottle [a plastic bottle kept in the tent for use at night and not to be mistaken for the water bottle]. He described how he had woken up bursting for a pee and had reached for the said bottle. Unscrewing the cap he had brought the bottle into his sleeping bag but forgot that between the bottle opening and his 'old fellow' was the relatively impermeable sleeping bag liner. His pee didn't prove powerful enough to force its way through the liner and a damp night ensued ....

The days are ticking by in a kind of time blur as we acclimatise and take care of the dozens of jobs that need doing before we can really get going on the mountain. Dick has given us the low-down on the oxygen equipment, which we probably won't use but have brought for both medical purposes and as a climbing back-up. It's such an effort to carry the heavy cylinders into place though, that it's hard to imagine that we'll use it — different if you have a chain of porters carrying the stuff to the high camps!

Personal equipment preparation is high on most people's list with crampon adjustment [so that they will fit on while wearing the thick over boots] proving to be a real problem. Everyone has their own way of coping — Hugh makes a totally new front bail from wire which looks like something made by Heath Robinson and has everyone shuddering and vowing not to rope up with him. Bruce scratches his

---

Shaun Norman scans the desolate Rongbuk moraine terraces for bharal, Himalayan wild sheep.

eye badly and gets a large patch over it. Juan, the Catalan deputy leader, comes over to watch his team's progress through our telescope and seeing Bruce with his eye patch says, 'Ha, a jealous husband aye?'

At 8 am on 11 August two Catalans and three Nepalis set out from camp six for the summit. For seven hours we watch them plugging knee- to thigh-deep along the ridge. But in that time they only climbed 700 feet and at 3 pm they were forced to give up and return to camp six.

In the afternoon a Japanese expedition arrived to check out our base camp site. They intended to attempt the north ridge and their leader, the hot-shot Hasegawa, would attempt to solo the Japanese direct route on the north face. They decided that our base camp was not as attractive as the Catalan one and moved back there, which made us wonder what the Catalans had that we didn't.

Everyone was looking forward to 13 August because the yaks were due to arrive to carry the gear up to advance base camp, and with luck a little further still. The Catalans had warned us to watch the yak drivers. 'They are very light-fingered,' warned Juan. When they arrived one could be forgiven for treating them with more than a little suspicion. They bore a remarkable similarity to their animals — hairy, unkempt, smelly and tough-looking — were dressed in a variety of clothing including baggy sheepskin pants, and had their thick black hair twisted into pigtails. Like almost every other Tibetan they wore a lump of turquoise in their left earlobe as insurance against being re-incarnated as a donkey. The yaks (and presumably naks, the female of the species) were set free to wander the barren hillsides in search of something to eat. So hairy were their bodies that it was impossible to tell their sex, but yak or nak they were the epitome of toughness. And looking at the vegetation of the country around base camp I could only marvel at their ability to find nourishment amongst the moraine and scree. If one were asked to design the ideal high-altitude animal, one would almost certainly come up with something closely resembling a yak. I wondered, only a little seriously, how long it would be before a yak reached the summit of Chomolungma.

The Tibetans pitched their old black tent which was soon filled to overflowing with the acrid smoke of burning dung. Then the herders shambled slowly through the camp peering into our tents like poor people looking into shop windows. In the evening Rob, Bruce and I paid a goodwill visit to their tent and partook of some local snuff. An hour-and-a-half later, as a result of his style of not doing things in half measures, Bruce staggered from the tent looking like a stoned owl, having sniffed enough snuff to put a yak on its back.

The yak drivers did not believe in early starts, probably because they were

---

Body language bridging the chasm between English and Tibetan. Austin Brookes announces an increase in yak payload to the head yak-herder.

'The Gang of Four', as our yak-herders were called, only sometimes with affection. Their working day started around 11 am, after a leisurely breakfast of yak-butter tea and snuff. By 5 pm their day was over and they were often to be found relaxing in our mess tent, paying close but mute attention to the activity around them.

normally paid by the day, so it was not until after midday that they got their hairy herd down for loading. Some of the animals lay down on the stones to await their fate, the younger ones stood friskily tossing their heads and swishing their busy tails, and some other older, more experienced ones rummaged through the old rubbish dumps, making a hell of a mess with cans and bottles that had only been buried under one layer of rocks. The herders loaded the animals with great circumspection, giving their horned heads a wide berth; we understood why when one tossing horn put a two-inch hole neatly through one of our metal cans. Austin moved about shouting encouragement, 'Ah, you're a lovely chap ... how's it going, smiley ... ah, you're a grisly old bugger!' He said everything with a big smile and to the non-English-speaking Tibetans it presumably all came across as good-natured banter.

About 1.30 pm our caravan set out for advance base camp, the yaks swaying slowly under their 120-pound loads while expedition members carried around 40 pounds. To begin with the route followed the rocky trough between the hillside

---

The north face looms over Changtse as Austin Brookes and Warwick Anderson heft loads over down-valley moraines between base camp and advance base camp.

Rob Blackburne's bread had just one failing: a crust which yielded cleanly only to the backsaw.

7

and the Rongbuk glacier. After about 2 miles we reached the valley of the East Rongbuk which came in on our left. The river was a raging brown fury, swollen by monsoon melt. Ross and Rob followed the yaks up to the higher crossing but the rest of us braved an old rope stretched across the narrow gorge. The crossing was a stimulating manoeuvre in an otherwise ordinary moraine bash. Each seemed to have his own way of dealing with the problem but basically it involved clipping yourself on to the rope with a carabiner and hauling yourself and your pack across, hand over hand, while the river raged past a few feet below. Austin's system was an interesting variation on everyone else's. He hung beneath the rope and pulled himself across with his hands but he let his legs do some of the work as well. They were wrapped around his pack and hauled it across behind him. He arrived with a comical look on his upside down face.

Beyond the East Rongbuk the route climbed up through the lateral moraines and then descended on to the rock-covered glacier. After a few hundred yards, which seemed much further, a vague path climbed 300 feet up the moraine wall and then sidled up and down to a grassy terrace with a little lake in the middle. It was an inspirational spot for a camp with superb views up the West Rongbuk

Over the brink and on to the glaciers: the view from the edge of advance base camp across the Rongbuk glacier pinnacles towards the West Rongbuk glacier in the background.

glacier. The peaks up there were not wildly spectacular (or was I becoming blase about spectacular views), more like peaks in New Zealand I thought than the really stimulating fluted peaks seen on the other side of the Himalaya. One peak, Pumori, was outstanding with its great white north face rising to a fiercely corniced summit ridge. On the far side of the flat, three tents represented the camp of the team being led by the French ace climber, Pierre Beghin, who with his wife, Annie, was attempting to climb the north face of Chomolungma. A fourth tent was that pitched by Steve and Hugh.

They greeted us cheerlessly and things didn't brighten up until Austin arrived much later, shouting his strange good-natured praise-and-abuse cocktail at the yak drivers. He then ripped the top off a bottle of Black Douglas whisky and called for everyone to come and share it with the French support group, Glynis, Dominique and Yannick. Glynis was the only non-French, but as a Canadian she spoke fluent French. We all immediately fell in love with her and her colonial sense of humour, to which we were introduced when she offered to swap camembert cheese for tinned kiwi, and then pretended to be Mrs Thatcher trying

Our route up the Rongbuk glacier from advance base camp followed the true right lateral moraine, then snuck deftly on to a medial moraine for the last stretch up to camp one. Fortunately, our route avoided close acquaintance with the ice pinnacles. (Ross Cullen)

to get New Zealand butter accepted by the European Economic Community.

The next day, 16 August, was a miserable grey day with rain and sleet at base camp and snow higher up. Despite the awful weather Dick, Ross, Rob and I decided to bring more gear up to advance base camp and, as so often happens, once we were under way we were glad to have made the effort. At advance base camp the atmosphere seemed to match the greyness of the day and I began to feel a division growing between Hugh and Steve as the young thrusters and the rest of us whom they perhaps saw as the old bulls. They were clearly keen to get moving up the mountain but it was obvious to the rest of us that there was much carrying to do before that could happen. On the way back to base we stopped at a large rock to do some 'bouldering' (difficult climbing close to the ground), before hurrying happily back to fresh hot bread baked by Shaun. We were acclimatising well.

Diary: 17 August. A rest day for the yaks before the final carry to ABC [advance base camp]. I act as base camp guard and cook while Ross and Rob visit Rongbuk monastery and the rest carry to ABC. After the usual household chores like cleaning up breakfast dishes and fetching water I try to do a recording to send home. The yak drivers peer at me from a few feet away, driving me frantic — quizzical looks on their faces as I spoke into the little magic box. Meanwhile the bread that Rob had lovingly made and left me in charge of burned, signalling the beginning of a bad day. One culinary disaster follows another and by the time the carriers returned I am in a right state. Then visitors begin to arrive, firstly one of the Catalan Nepalis called Kali returning from the north ridge. He is a very slight, well-spoken character who is losing his face as sheets of burnt skin peel off. I give him a cup of tea and biscuits and question him about himself. He is an ex-student of one of Ed Hillary's schools and Kathmandu University, and is a lawyer turned high-altitude porter. I challenge his claim that he is a Sherpa and he admits he is really a Tamang — a tough group who like Sherpas are ethnically Tibetan and who were once, in fact, a group of Tibetan cavalry. Kali is followed by a constant stream of French, Catalans and trekkers of unknown origin. On the food scene it's an effort but somehow Rob, Ross and I coped. On the radio at 8 pm we hear that Steve and Hugh have carried a load up to a site for camp one on the Rongbuk glacier opposite the west spur. The Catalans have withdrawn from the mountain. After a rest they will give it one last shot but are having difficulty remaining confident.

I awoke in the early hours of 18 August to the sound of the Toyota's motor gassing out the camp. Warwick had been dashing about the camp for hours, first finishing a newspaper article and then getting gear together for the trip down country to post the article to New Zealand. Thankfully, at 6 am the Toyota left with Mr Chan, James and Warwick. A few hours later in an atmosphere of tense expectation the

team, except for Hugh, Steve and Warwick, gathered in the big tent to hear Austin announce the climbing teams and their jobs in the immediate future. Bruce Farmer would lead Hugh Van Noorden, Mike Andrews and Dick Price; Mike Rheinberger's team was Peter Allen, Steve Bruce and Mike Perry; mine was Rob Blackburne, Ross Cullen and Shaun Norman. (Nicknames gradually emerged for the three climbing teams — Itchycrutch, Pissbowl, Groupie — based on idiosyncrasies of single individuals in each team. The two reserves, Austin and Warwick, who were ready to stand in should they be needed in any of the teams, named themselves 'spare parts' but we soon changed that to 'private parts'. These slightly derogatory names were all good innocent fun to begin with, especially in my own team, but understandably many began to get sensitive about their names and we comfortably slipped into a more up-market image — Bruce Farmer's team became Team Comalco, Mike Rheinberger's Team Fairydown and mine Team Toyota, in recognition of three of our major sponsors. 'Private parts' had no pretensions and remained 'private parts', but then later on Warwick joined Team Fairydown and

The yaks and drivers at the dump. After advance base camp the yaks dropped precariously down on to the glacier, and all went well until, after about one hour of yak travel, the herders mysteriously called the caravan to an abrupt halt. This was the end of the road for the yaks but why was not apparent. The yaks were easily capable of reaching camp one. Curiously, the French had their dump a few minutes down glacier and, later, the Japanese had their dump forty minutes up glacier. (Mike Andrews)

Austin was left alone in the support group.) Austin announced at the meeting that the plum job of having the first go at the west spur should fall to my team. It was a pity Steve and Hugh weren't there because this exacerbated the problem that was growing between them and the rest of the group.

We tried in vain to get the yak drivers moving early. At lunchtime Austin and Bruce began to negotiate with Pine Tree over payment for the yaks. The Tibetans were claiming the standard eleven days at 59 yuan per day, covering the cost of yak, driver and food. Everyone else apparently paid this inflated rate but not the New Zealanders, as Pine Tree soon learned. Austin put the case succinctly and moved out to leave Bruce to battle away; it was a tried and tested technique which they were expert at using. Pine Tree was caught in the middle, wanting to please the Chinese Mountaineering Association (who wanted to keep on good terms with the Tibetans) but also wanting to please us, his clients. Bruce argued convincingly like a union advocate, trying to get Pine Tree on his side: 'Now Pine Tree, we can see that you have been left in a difficult situation. ... We must not allow these Tibetans to drive a wedge between us. ... You know we have no objection to the CMA making a profit. ...' It was a brilliant performance. Much later the final agreement was for only seven days' pay.

The yaks were finally loaded and away by 1.30 pm, just as Austin collapsed with a violent attack of dysentery. It was my job to follow the yaks and keep an eye on their light-fingered owners. At the climb up to the animal ford in the East Rongbuk I got a little behind and the Tibetans must have thought that I had gone across the rope and that they were alone, because as I rounded a corner near the top of the hill I came across one of the Tibetans guiltily holding a coil of rope. Two hundred feet below him was a second coil where presumably the one in his hands was about to go as well. I was furious and breathlessly assaulted him with a tirade of bad language that would have made a trooper blush, but it bridged the language gap and he leapt over the side and soon had the rope back. Meanwhile a similar barrage of obscenities stopped the other yak drivers who were a few hundred yards away. By the time we reached the river my anger had abated a little. The yaks tottered across the brown torrent with remarkable stability. The Tibetans all removed their baggy pants and then linked together we waded through the almost waist-deep water. Probably their first wash since their wedding night I thought.

At advance base camp Steve and Hugh were unhappy not to be included in the first action on the mountain but in deference to the plan they left next morning for camp one. Austin had decided for the sake of peace to allow them to reconnoitre the route to the foot of the spur.

On 20 August, Rob, Ross, Dick, Mike Perry and I set out to carry a load to camp one. The route sidled off the upper end of the advance base camp terrace

---

Eventually we wore a path between advance base camp and camp one. What in the early days had been a formidable slog became, in time, a pleasant amble. The moraine quickly shredded our running shoes but the pleasure of walking beneath Chomolungma's satellite peaks endured. Seen in the background here is Changtse.

CABIN

and after several hundred yards descended the moraine wall to the glacier. Suddenly we were in another world. A world of giant white ice pinnacles rose like ghostly forms from the soft mist. It was like being in a white forest. After walking up the glacier ice for thirty minutes we came to the dump, the place where the yaks had dumped gear and food intended for the upper camps. Here Rob and I couldn't contain ourselves and climbed one of the pinnacles while Mike photographed enthusiastically.

From the dump the route climbed tediously through moraine for just over a mile before ascending a snowy trough between ice walls for a few hundred yards. Camp one was situated on a small flat on the glacier where the Rongbuk divided into four: to the east a small glacier flowed down from the steep west face of Changtse; to the west of the Rongbuk one broad glacier flowed gently down from the Lho La pass between the west spur of Chomolungma and the peak of Khumbutse; another glacier tumbled down from the white wedge of Lingtren; and the Rongbuk itself did a big sweeping turn to the east disappearing behind Changtse. Towering overhead was the massive pyramid of Chomolungma — the north ridge on the left, the west ridge on the right with the great north face between.

It was 2.30 pm and just as we arrived Hugh and Steve left without a word to us to mark the route across the glacier. We were all a bit shocked at their lack of communication. Dick said quietly, 'A brew would have been nice.' I was a little more vocal and shouted furiously after them, 'Are you bastards part of this team?' Despite this we were all very happy and were soon chattering enthusiastically over a cup of tea. We could hear the south-westerly roaring over the top, 10,000 feet above, and a few avalanches crashed down. The steep and narrow Hornbein Couloir was the focus of our concentration, it was certainly the crux of the west ridge route.

'Not much higher than the Caroline face, from here to the top,' said Mike.

'Yeah ... what a shame we're not that fit.'

On the way down we built dozens of cairns and generally tidied up the route, and to finish off a good day we went scavenging in the old Japanese and British dumps led by the human magpie Doctor Dick. Most of us lost interest after a minor find or two, but Dick knew a bargain when he smelled one and burrowed vehemently for rope, primuses and canned food.

Back at advance base camp Pierre and Annie Beghin had returned from their attempt on the north face. They had reached 26,000 feet in the Great Gully before being defeated by deep snow. They had then descended to their camp two before climbing up to the north ridge. Pierre, a cool customer with rugged film-star looks, described how they climbed as if on 'egg shells' because the snow slopes on the north ridge proved very dangerous. From the north ridge they had intended to climb to the top but were surprised to find the Catalans still there. They had expected them to be finished. The Catalans, of course, didn't want the Beghins stealing their thunder so there was nothing for it but to descend. All the while

---

Team motivator and strongman Bruce Farmer indulges his weakness for Chinese sun bonnets at advance base camp.

that Pierre was talking, the attractive Annie, dressed in a fashionable bright pink duvet, interrupted incessantly in French. My diary records: 'Pierre is being sponsored by a diamond merchant to make a solo ascent of Everest by a new route. ... Their impression of us is that because we wear funny hats and striped longjohns we don't take mountaineering seriously, and that we lack any real powerhouses to push the route through — contrast perhaps to some expeditions that comprise nothing but prima donnas, so much so that they are incapable of working as a team.'

The next evening Steve and Hugh came down and I decided to air my grievances with them. In a really frank discussion they told us that they felt they were the only ones fit enough to be out in front. Rheinberger said, 'There are twelve other fit buggers keen to get out in front — Bruce Farmer has been carrying 80-pound loads from base camp to ABC.' Everyone seemed happy to have had their say and thankfully the air was cleared. The only possible area left for conflict later seemed to be the approach we would use above camp three. Steve and Hugh appeared to favour a light, fast push over the final 5,000 feet, whereas the rest of us preferred a more solid build-up that would give a greater number of people a chance for the top in reasonable safety.

Is it a strategic conference or is Bruce Farmer just explaining the intricacies of the aluminium industry?

'Red sky at night: shepherd's delight,' but not for us. Clear skies here but over two feet of fresh avalanche snow.

Pierre and Annie Beghin (Shaun Norman) *and Glynis* (Warwick Anderson).

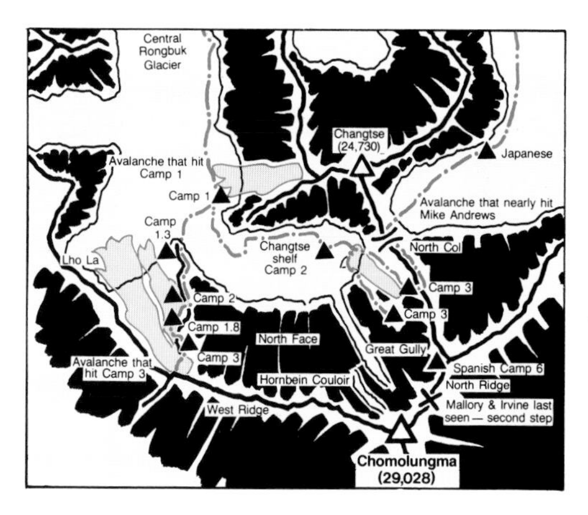

The monomaniacal attitude required to climb Chomolungma can be so depressing if you are an explorer at heart.

On the afternoon of 21 August, Shaun and Ross went to camp one and next day, while they crossed the glacier for a look at the spur, Rob and I tramped up to camp one. They arrived back looking tired after failing to reach the foot of the spur and with a depressing story of dangerous snow conditions.

Next morning dawned cold and misty with a few flakes of snow in the air but we were not to be put off. By 10.15 am we were clipped into some flashy new Nordic skis and skinning across the glacier towards the spur, which remained hidden in the mist. At the dump of gear left by Shaun and Ross the day before we stood peering into the mist, hoping for a break and feeling extremely vulnerable as the muffled sounds of avalanches echoed about the valley. It would have been very easy to turn back and wait for a fine day but I really had the bit between my teeth and led on up to the left. After a few hundred feet we came to a huge gaping bergschrund. Rob and I took off our skis and climbed up on to a narrow bridge which seemed to give access to snow slopes that led up to the spur. It was exciting to be getting some real climbing and we felt invigorated balancing over the seracs and narrow bridges. Then a clearing of the mist revealed an easier alternative, so Shaun and Ross carried the skis a little further up the glacier to the new start point while Rob and I pushed on up the slope towards an old rope hanging above. It was thin and fragile but we pulled it from the snow and followed it up to a band of loose rock. This we clambered up for a couple of hundred feet, fixing some new rope as we went. The final steep snow gully led to the corniced crest. I clambered over the bulge and on to the spur with a feeling of great triumph — we had struck the first blow and had a real foothold on the 'hill'.

Full moon, gas lantern — camp one beneath Chomolungma.

The ski-run home was made terrible by bad snow and zero visibility. At one place I had crashed and was in a compromising position kneeling with my face between my skis, when Ross streaked past inches away and crashed in a similar posture just in front.

'Christ that was close, you just about reamed me with a ski.'

'Yeah ... I think I've broken my bloody binding,' he moaned.

On the radio we learned that Waka had returned from an epic and frustrating trip to the fleshpots. My diary records simply 'no bloody mail'.

We were woken in the morning by Shaun's shout that a brew was on the way. We struggled out of our sleeping bags and crowded into his tent for a breakfast of porridge and muesli — together! I could hardly eat it at sea level not to mention at 19,000 feet at dawn, but somehow it went down. The weather wasn't much better than the day before but stoically we plodded across to our skis. The day before I had been unstoppable but now it felt like sheer drudgery, a job that just had to be done. I shuffled across the white wilderness far behind the others, cursing

Shaun Norman makes a dawn start from camp one, Khumbutse (left) and Lingtren (right) behind. We used a mixture of alpine and three-pin skis for travel up the glacier. Invariably, ski conditions were superb in the morning as we slogged uphill, but by evening when we descended, the conditions had changed to breakable crust and 'porridge'. (Ross Cullen)

my ski bindings as they came off every few paces, 'frigging French crap'. Eventually sheer frustration motivated me to fix the problem, which gave me a feeling of satisfaction at being able to perform the repair with only my Swiss Army pocket-knife. Shaun got to the foot of the fixed ropes first but, not able to control his enthusiasm, he skied down whooping and yelling as he carved graceful telemark turns. Grunting up the slope I was unreasonably angry that he was using his energy this way rather than with the job in hand.

At the bergschrund we changed skis for crampons and set off. I moved five paces and felt almost asphyxiated by the heat; stopping suddenly I realised I was in front again, 'damn it!' We climbed the snow slope and loose rock slowly to where the fixed rope ended, tied to a couple of rock pegs. From here, with Ross belaying the rope I trailed, I climbed the steep snow to the cornices. Here I found a small hole into which I crawled. Beyond the curtain of icicles the hole expanded into a large cavern, a perfect shelter.

Above the cavern we clambered on to a level part of the spur where heaps of wind slab avalanche debris made us less than enthusiastic about the slopes above. Shaun fixed the reel of rope he was carrying to an ice axe and began up the slope.

Climbers at camp one-point-three and on the fixed rope below. (Warwick Anderson)

I plugged behind him to near the avalanche break and then he belayed me as, with heart in mouth, I began up the dangerous slope. I climbed as near the crest as I could, ready to dive down the other side if the hollow-sounding snow did take off. After 150 feet I put in a runner and, feeling a little safer, climbed on to the ridge above looking for a place to anchor the end of the rope. A big spike provided the answer and I took the rope from my harness, tied a loop in it and dropped it over the spike. Once untied from the rope I became suddenly conscious of the horrendous drop down to the Rongbuk on my left and for the first time noticed the storm which had blown up while I was engrossed in climbing. As the wind pelted me with particles of snow and ice I wrapped the rope around my body and slid quickly back to my friends. A few moments later we were back inside the calm of the ice cave eating scroggin. When we re-emerged the Jekyll and Hyde day had become Jekyll again and the sun shone strongly from a blue sky. Above us the great pyramid of Chomolungma looked just as remote as ever.

We quickly abseiled down the ropes and skied back to camp one where Rheinberger's group, Team Fairydown, were waiting eager to relieve us. After a

A sloth's eye-view of mundane domesticity. Sheltered in the warmth of a sleeping bag within the flaps of his tent, the photographer captures Australians Peter Allan and Mike Rheinberger pegging their underwear out on the shrouds of the advance base camp radio aerial in defiance of an impending snow storm.

brew Rob, Ross and I set off down, leaving behind Shaun who wanted to visit the Lho La before descending. At the dump we met Mike Andrews and from there, despite our tired bodies, the journey home to advance base camp was done at top speed. Mike is a very quiet character but can be incredibly competitive when he is wound up. We crested the top of the moraine wall at 100 miles an hour, with Rob in front followed by me, Mike and Ross. The pace was getting steadily faster until we turned the corner 150 yards from the camp. Mike broke first and suddenly it was an all out sprint with line honours going to Rob. We all collapsed inside the cook tent, sucking air in furiously and laughing like kids.

Next morning we shared a brew with Glynis and Yannick, her boyfriend. Glynis was as lyrical as ever. Between mouthfuls of our fruitcake (swapped for camembert) she said, 'The Catalans can't imagine how Reinhold Messner could get up the Big E. by himself.'

'Yeah, but Reinhold had the beautiful Nena with him,' retorted a New Zealander.

Suddenly Glynis switched to being Nena, reclining on the East Rongbuk with

---

Austin Brookes on the fixed rope, and three hundred feet below is camp one-point-three. A trip up the fixed ropes guaranteed exhaustion, but for many of us the slog was transcended by the contest between light and cloud. (Warwick Anderson)

---

a megaphone, 'Come on Reinhold ... go for it Reinhold. ...'

Diary: 25 August. Rob, Ross and I descend to base camp for a break. Rob cooks a beautiful loaf of bread and we deliver it to the Catalans who are about to launch their offensive. The Beghins are also going up again for a final go.
26th. A lovely rest day — sleep in, wash in hot water and eat heaps. A letter has arrived from Sorrel. She still hasn't managed to buy a donkey but as we suggested she has already given it the name 'Budget'.

Late on 26 August we set off again. Feeling drugged and sleepy after a wonderful rest at base camp we weaved over the endless moraine to advance base camp. Shaun had stayed at advance base camp and was the only one in residence. He too looked well rested. On the hill, Team Fairydown had pushed on with the route and had fixed rope a few hundred feet higher. They had also established an intermediate camp that they called 'one point three' on the flat ridge just above the ice grotto. It wasn't my idea of a safe place, particularly when there was a perfectly good crevasse only 50 feet away, but they obviously thought it was safe enough.

Meanwhile the Catalans mounted their final attempt on Chomolungma. Two teams of six plugged up to the top camp at 27,500 feet. There were three Nepalis and three Catalans in each team and to counter the soft snow they were divided into Team A and Team B. It was Team B's job to plug steps along the top ridge as far as they could, so that the next day Team A could go through to the top. Early on 28 August Team B set out. When Rob looked through the telescope at 10.30 am, they had just reached the foot of the 'second step' and were clearly going to do quite well. However, above the step (now made easy by the old Chinese ladder and ropes) the snow remained deep and the going very soft. At 6.20 pm they completed the task for Team A but plugged on to the summit. Even on that wind-blown peak they were knee-deep in snow. The descent was a nightmare as tired limbs refused to co-ordinate properly in the snowy mire. At 9 pm, still above the second step, they sat down, their oxygen-starved brains refusing to drive them any further.

The Nepalis, however, were still in reasonably good shape and two of them set off down to get some oxygen left on the ridge below. From base camp Juan was keeping a radio vigil, talking to Team B almost continuously through the night, encouraging them to stay alive. To begin with, the four on the ridge had sat alone in their misery, little islands of exhaustion waiting to die. But Juan encouraged them to huddle together. Then he spoke to Carlos who was in very bad shape.

'Carlos, your pregnant wife will have your son tomorrow.'

'I don't care ... if we don't get oxygen, we'll die,' replied Carlos.

Later when we were told about the radio marathon, Rob said, 'Austin and Bruce couldn't keep us alive like that.'

'Why not?'

'Because we can't afford the batteries!' Incredibly, the Nepalis got back to their friends with the oxygen at 11 am the next day. They spent three hours reviving, and at 2 pm they all started down, reaching camp six at about 9 pm.

After this near disaster Team A's attempt was cancelled and when one keen Catalan announced his intention of making a solo summit bid the leader ordered his gear to be taken away from him. Like many successful attempts on Chomolungma this one had in the end walked so close to the brink of disaster that the outcome depended finally on just a throw of the dice, and the leader had decided that enough was enough. They would, after all, return to Catalonia as public heroes who had pulled off a wonderful victory, but we wondered how much credit the Nepalis would get for their incredible feat of strength and endurance.

Pierre and Annie had now joined the Catalan team on the north ridge, hoping to snatch the summit in the wake of the Catalans' success but as they left camp five, Pierre set off a small avalanche which swept Annie down 250 feet, so they called off their attempt. Meanwhile on the west spur, Steve Bruce and Rheinberger, supported by Peter Allan and Mike Perry, had pushed the ropes up to 22,000 feet before handing over to Team Comalco.

For Shaun, Rob, Ross and me the next few days were devoted to carrying from advance base camp to camp one. Despite the potential drudgery of the task we enjoyed ourselves enormously. The day of 29 August was no exception. We had walked up the glacier and past the forest of ice pinnacles, while wreaths of mist swirled around the 'penitentes' giving the place an unworldly atmosphere. The heavy loads we had picked up from the dump and the grind up off the white ice quietened down our enthusiastic chatter for a while, but then once the going levelled off through the moraine Ross led an economics argument about whether or not people should be charged to enter national parks in New Zealand. This lasted twenty minutes until Rob began to increase the pace in the trough leading to camp one. I was still smarting over being beaten into advance base camp several days before, so tucked myself in behind Rob and concentrated on my breathing. One hundred yards from camp I made my break and burst into the lead with a shrieking war cry, but Rob accelerated immediately and we spent the next 50 yards elbowing, shouldering and ankle tapping each other. Thus we arrived at camp in a state of advanced exhaustion and spent the next ten minutes in spasms of laughter and sucking thin air. Mike Perry turned to us with a slightly sorrowful look and said, 'Don't you guys take anything seriously?'

By the time we got back to advance base camp we had more or less recovered but worse was to come. You've heard about the last supper, but, gentle Christians, have you heard about the worst supper? When we entered the kitchen tent at about 5 pm Mike Perry was ensconced behind a bank of primuses. He may not have intended to cook dinner but when Team Toyota entered and sat down hungrily on the kerosene tins in the meal position he was more or less trapped. At the time he was juggling a brick-sized lump of dough to which he would occasionally add flour, then juggle and knead some more.

'Anyone seen the salt?' asked Mike.

'You don't need much' said Ross tossing him the bag of salt.

After a while I asked, 'What would be the chances of a brew?' but Mike clearly had his hands full so I made a billy of coffee.

'Seen the milk powder, Mike?'

'Yeah, here.' He threw me the bag of white powder which I poured into the coffee. Yuck, it was flour!

'What'll I cook for dinner?' asked Mike. Several suggestions were tossed nonchalantly his way as he continued kneading the brick-sized lump. Occasionally he would make a hole in it into which he would pour flour. Ross put a tape on the music machine. Some old rock began to play.

'What sort of music is that?' someone asked.

'Little Feat Live,' said Ross defensively, 'best of the seventies, boy!' Everyone sipped their coffee, Mike finished kneading and hung a billy with the brick in it from the roof of the tent. It stayed there for a moment and then fell with a crash, narrowly missing his head.

'Bugger!' exclaimed Mike. 'What'll I cook for dinner?' he asked again. Two hours had now elapsed and this time several ingredients were thrust forcefully at him. By now the boys had turned into more a stunned audience than hungry mountaineers, and beneath the good-humoured chatter was growing an hysteria fired by hunger and frustration. Shaun was the first to crack and went to bed.

A wide-ranging argument-cum-discussion followed and then some insensitive fool asked, 'OK you guys, whose got Rheinbuggle's ice axe?' (referring to Mike's ice axe that had disappeared from camp one a couple of days before). Most people pulled funny faces and made silly comments and Ross suggested getting Steve Bruce, the policeman, on to the case. Rheinberger's reaction to all this humour at his expense was a vigorous chastisement of everyone in the tent. 'I wish you buggers would take this more seriously ... when I leave an item of equipment in a particular place I expect to find it there.' The radio at 8 pm relieved the pregnant silence that followed.

Meanwhile Mike Perry had poured a packet of sauce-mix into some hot water but after beating it with disinterest he announced it inedible and put it to one side. The same fate befell a billyful of vermicelli and he was soon 'sautéing' (so he called it) a few bits of green pepper in some lukewarm fat. But on a more hopeful note he put the brick on to cook again. Then things really started to look up. Mike produced some soup and Shaun got out of bed to drink it. After the soup I looked hopefully at the grey matter that had begun life as a French packet-sauce and asked, 'Who'd eat some of this if I doctored it up?' An encouraging but unenthusiastic murmur which sounded like death moans filled the tent and Shaun went to bed again. I added a few spices and potato flakes and some of the more adventurous souls ate the concoction without joy. I then tried to resurrect the

---

Rob Blackburne and Graeme Dingle en route to camp one. (Ross Cullen)

A first view of Khumbutse above the cloud-darkened seracs of the Rongbuk glacier, from the trail between advance base camp and camp one. The mountain has its storm cap on.

---

vermicelli but that was asking a bit too much. Meanwhile Mike Perry knocked the lamp over and cut his finger trying to fix it.

We had now been waiting for dinner for over five hours but we clung to one final hope, the chef's *coup de grâce,* the bread. At 10.05 pm Mike opened the billy and produced a very solid brick-like loaf. It didn't appear to have increased in size at all but I sawed off a few bits and Rob spread on butter and jam. 'Perhaps it tastes better than it looks,' I mumbled. Rob and I took tentative little bites while watching each other carefully for some reaction. We both spluttered together — 'God, there's too much salt, it tastes terrible' — and the hysteria that had been building up for several hours exploded. Rob was clutching his ribs and looked as if he was having an apoplectic fit. I took on the same attitude but then lost my balance and fell sideways off the kerosene tin into the corner of the tent. Then I became aware that only Rob and I were laughing. I sneaked a look up at Mike. There was no expression of amusement on his face whatsoever, instead he was staring ahead, his eyes glazed over with the look of a shocked and broken man. With the utmost embarrassment I crawled through the tent door into the night and retreated to my sleeping bag. Before we left for camp one in the morning Rob and I with cap in hand went to Mike and apologised.

It was our turn in front again. Dick and Hugh had established a camp at about 22,000 feet that they had called 'one point eight' because it was not an ideal site for camp two. Our job was to establish camp two and then go on and find a site for camp three. With these goals in mind we climbed slowly up to camp one-point-three on 2 September, concerned about what we would find at the camp because above us ravens were having great fun flying out over the cliffs with biscuits and other goodies in their beaks.

The lone Chrysalis tent at the camp was a depressing sight. Strewn around it in a 15-yard arc were the remains of the ravens' party. Half-eaten packets of food littered the snow. The tent door flapped gently in the breeze.

'Don't those bastards know how to zip up a tent?' I moaned at no one in particular. Rob eyed a big black raven squatting on the snow 30 feet away.

'These buggers have probably been into the local toilets as well as the sky burial,'* he groaned with distaste as he hurled half-eaten bits of food over the side. Shaun made a brew, then we pitched another Chrysalis and as the evening clouds began playing around Changtse we crawled into our sleeping bags and began to melt snow for drinks and food.

The sky was dark and ominous next morning as we climbed the steep snow spur. The old steps were obliterated by new snow and had to be replugged. The

*The sky burial is the traditional Tibetan way of disposing of the dead. The body is cut up, crushed and mixed with tsampa (barley flour), and then fed to the birds. The locals believe in this way the spirit is freed.

Dick Price putting the finishing touches to camp one-point-eight. A few days later, on 5 October, at 16 minutes past midnight to be precise, our conviction that we were on a relatively safe route suffered a mortal blow. Two hundred feet above one-point-eight a complex strata of windslabs sheared off to a depth of about 6 feet. In an instant camp one-point-eight disintegrated, the entire snowcave slid off and the tent which was firmly tied to the fixed rope, was shredded. (Hugh Van Noorden)

fixed rope was frozen in too, and had to be laboriously hauled to the surface. For the first thousand feet or so I was happy to let the others do the hard work but one can only shirk for so long and beneath a steep dangerous-looking face I found myself on the sharp end again. I climbed in short quick anaerobic bursts of five, ten, fifteen and twenty steps, giving myself little objectives each time. A couple of times I even got up to twenty-five steps before I had to stop for a couple of minutes in preparation for another burst. I was concerned that my progress would release the new snow hanging at an alarming angle all around us, so I tried to stick to a small rib where it was a little more consolidated but this was at odds with the fixed rope which traversed the open slope and Shaun, annoyed by this, was hurling obscenities up at me, presumably because he thought I was being eccentric. I was relieved to reach the corniced crest where the slope fell back to a safer angle. Two hundred feet away I could make out a hole in the slope which I hoped would lead to the new camp two. Rob joined me and together we plugged up to it, eager to see what lay beneath. I clambered inside the freezing chamber and was immediately enthusiastic about what I found. Twenty feet down I turned left into the bowels of a crevasse where great icicles hung like organ pipes all twisted and distorted by the ever-creeping ice. A jumble of huge ice blocks littered the floor. To the left, however, was a small bench that could be enlarged to form a sleeping platform. Conditions on the spur were very dangerous and I was determined that camp two would be underground: this crevasse seemed to fit the bill perfectly. I climbed back out into the brilliant light and announced to Rob that we had found camp two, 'Pukerua'.

Shaun arrived still moaning about my inferior track-making and a few moments later we were all underground hacking out the sleeping bench in our new home. It was a quite weird place with great scrolls of ice weighing many tons jammed above our heads: they looked precarious but we figured they had been there a long time and it would be very bad luck if they chose the weeks that we were around to fall in. The walls were covered with awful and ferocious-looking gargoyles in the shapes of various animals: one was a duck-billed platypus running for its life, another looked like a sleeping bison. There was also a very cute-looking hippopotamus and a whole lot of ghosts and phantoms. Yes, it was a weird home but under the circumstances very safe and comfortable.

Next day we had several jobs to do to consolidate our position. While Ross and I built a weatherproof igloo-type entrance into Pukerua, Rob and Shaun carried up some rope that was hanging on a snow stake 300 feet below. This was to be more valuable to us than we could imagine a few days later. In the afternoon we sat on the terrace beside the new entrance munching on some scroggin and looking lazily across the peaks of Khumbutse, Lingtren and Pumori. What a wonderful time Shipton and his friends must have had in 1935 exploring those glaciers and climbing the peaks and passes — the monomaniacal attitude required to climb Chomolungma can be so depressing if you are an explorer at heart. Below us the Rongbuk glacier

---

Warwick Anderson, head bowed with tiredness, on the last stretch to camp two (Pukerua).

looked very broken as it drained from the basin formed by Changtse, the North Col, the north face and the west ridge of Chomolungma. While we looked, an avalanche poured down off the west ridge and spread lazily out on to the glacier.

That evening we listened to the BBC on Shaun's little transistor radio and heard about the celebration in Lhasa of the twentieth anniversary of Tibet's becoming a so-called 'Autonomous Region'. And in New Zealand things were hotting up over the French bombing of the Greenpeace flagship *Rainbow Warrior*. Tongue-in-cheek we declared that all French words were banned from conversation and were surprised at just how many Gallic words were in common mountaineering use. I went to sleep as Ross pretended to be President Reagan. In that familiar Californian drawl he was saying, 'Did the earth move for you Nancy ...?

I had the primuses going by 5.30 am on 3 September. The temperature in the crevasse was a relatively warm -8°C. A couple of brews of coffee, a bowl of muesli and a quick squat in the 'other part' of the crevasse and we were flogging up the hill again. A colourless dawn forced out the night without spectacle as we moved like automatons: kick, kick and move the protecting jumar up the fixed rope ... kick, kick and move the jumar. We could have just about done it in our sleep. Five or six hundred feet above Pukerua we reached the precarious-looking camp that Dick and Hugh had pitched. A Chrysalis tent clung to a ledge below a big sheltering rock and to the right was a small snow cave that they had dug. We picked up a little extra gear and food and continued on. At about 22,500 feet the fixed rope ended and we decided that the angle was easy enough not to need any more. Every twenty-five paces or so we left a marker wand, as the spur now became quite broad and could be difficult to follow in bad visibility. It was hard work plugging up the soft unconsolidated snow and the heat and thin air combined to make us feel as weak as walrus widdle. Rob was in good form and plugged away tirelessly until at about 23,000 feet I had to contrive a rest.

'Like a drink?' I managed to squeak between desperate breaths. I was thankful when he said 'yes' and sat down in the snow.

'Like some Elizabeth Hardon?' he grinned offering me his tube of suncream.

'No, but do you know why Elizabeth Arden was smiling?'

'No.'

'Because Max Factor.' At 23,000 feet it didn't have to be very funny to make us clutch our sides and roll around.

From our resting point we scanned the slope above and agreed it looked 'pretty hairy' but somewhere up there camp three had to go. We climbed another 500 or 600 feet to a point immediately below the final slope up to the west ridge and there we pitched the VE 24 and thankfully crawled in out of the heat. It was a bad place for a camp but it was the best of a bad lot. The only alternative was to go on to the exposed west ridge 400 feet above, which in retrospect may have been the best thing to do but, as we all know, hindsight is blind wisdom. Only

---

Warwick Anderson one step away from the frigid pleasures of Pukerua. Behind Warwick are Pumori (left) and Cho Oyu (centre).

---

when we came to descend did we realise just how dangerous the snow on the spur really was. In contrast to the ascent a cool drizzle swirled around us and we sank knee- to thigh-deep in the snow. Considering the steep angle it was suicidal stuff but we made Pukerua safely and were soon cocooned in our sleeping bags drinking a brew and feeling proud of having efficiently and quickly completed our task.

On the 8 pm radio sched Bruce told us the mail had come in.

'There's eleven for Rob, six for Ding, four for Ross and three for Shaun.'

'Any for me?' asked Rheinberger at camp one.

'Yeah, two.'

'Who from?'

'Hang on, I'll check. ...'

Shaun looked grim and said, 'Bad move ... Rheinbuggles is desperate for one from his girlfriend.'

Bruce came back on the radio breathing heavily, 'One from J. Rheinberger and one from Richard Long.' There was a very flat 'thank you' from Mike, confirming Shaun's fears.

A sloppy stew concocted from a variety of dehy. packets ended a good day and we were soon in the land of ziz. At 12.16 am a hideous roar shook the ice around us savagely and we all sat bolt upright. Shaun threw his arms around Ross, my arms shot out of the small face-hole in my sleeping bag and several voices simultaneously shouted the obvious, 'Avalanche!' For a very long dark and lonely fifteen seconds the roar continued to shake the ice, then all was silent. Shaun said quietly, 'I felt like a bloody trapped miner for a while.' I pulled on my boots and climbed up to inspect the damage. Our beautiful igloo entrance was completely gone, along with Shaun's ice axe which had been by the door. Most amazing of all, a snow stake which had been driven in up to the hilt in the snow inside the entrance, together with a long rope hanging from it into the crevasse, to which had been tied my crampons, had all been drawn out and taken away. We could only imagine the extent of the damage to the fixed rope, we guessed it would be substantial. There was nothing for it but to go back to sleep, but it wasn't easy. It didn't take much imagination to realise our situation was serious: we were virtually out of food; the weather was now bad and more snow would mean more avalanches; we had no crampons between us because all except mine had been left at camp three, and only three ice axes since Shaun's had been swept away; and for good measure the fixed rope below us had almost certainly been swept away. It was, however, an exciting feeling, a big challenge that somehow epitomised what the game was all about.

At 9 am Rob turned on the radio. 'Pukerua to one, over.'

'Roger Rob, over.'

After the avalanche at Pukerua, Mike Perry met Toyota during their descent. 'In the now thoroughly unwelcome afternoon snowstorm, we crossed paths with Toyota on the fixed rope. They looked drawn, dark rings under their eyes telling their story more eloquently than words.'

'We had a bit of excitement last night, over.'

'Yeah, go ahead, over.'

'An express train went over our heads ... the 12.16 to Rongbuk.'

'Hell, we heard the roar down here ... you guys all right?'

'Yeah, we're nearly out of food ... we'll come down as soon as the weather clears.'

Outside it was snowing and windy again and a thick mist made it impossible to see more than 20 feet. Inside Pukerua we built a wall to stop cascading snow building up on the sleeping bench and then we got into a serious game of scrabble. It was a cool -6°C but with a slight breeze stirring the air it felt much colder so we played with our sleeping bags drawn up around our noses and big mitts on our hands, and the stakes were high — the loser had to go out and check the weather.

'What's a guy who grows pecans called, a pecaneer?' asked Shaun.

'What the hell is a pecan?' asked the rest of us. Then Rob put down HIAM.

'My god, what is a bloody HIAM?'

'You know,' said Rob sheepishly, 'that part of the vagina.'

'What part of the vagina ... that's the bloody hymen!' Hysteria followed. I was allowed SIEVER (someone who uses a sieve) after much discussion. Ross was caught with four 'U's and tried to put down 'UCUUUNT', but that was definitely disallowed. Finally Rob had to check the weather and announced no change. Dinner was a watery brew and a couple of pills to help us sleep.

I awoke shortly after dawn and peered up at the shaft of light piercing the deep blue of the crevasse, trying to work out whether it was the light of a fine day. It was impossible to tell so I struggled out of my warm bag and into my boots and climbed up to the entrance. 'Eureka!' It was a fine day. We prepared ourselves casually and left the cave at 10.30 am carrying all the fixed rope and snow stakes.

The amount of new snow that had built up was frightening and loitering was definitely not in the plan. The fixed rope had been swept into the gully to the west of the spur and was so tight that you could just about play a tune on it. I fixed another rope and cut the old one free, and then Shaun abseiled down and managed to retrieve 200 feet. We then fixed the new rope as we abseiled down. After we had descended 700 feet Shaun slid down to me and handed over the final 200 feet that he had recovered from the gully. I fixed it to a snow stake, threw it down, and then looked at Shaun, 'If we can't reach some of the old fixed rope with this abseil, we're in the shit old son.' I then slid off down. The old Dingle luck prevailed, however — 3 feet from the end of the abseil the fixed rope started again. I clipped into it with a feeling of great relief and traversed left to the arete. But then the really hard work began. The rope was buried 3 feet into the snow and had to be laboriously hauled and hacked out. It was an exhausting effort but eventually we were stumbling down the slope to the forlorn-looking tents at camp one-point-three. Rob looked at me and said 'You look absolutely fucked.' We all lay in the snow and were soon laughing again. It was good to be alive.

Next day Team Fairydown began their own fateful climb to camp three, described in chapter one.

For us, the old argument about storms at full moon was finally resolved. Both our full moons were on clear nights but frustratingly we weren't in a position to exploit these opportunities.

Chapter 7 *The North Face*

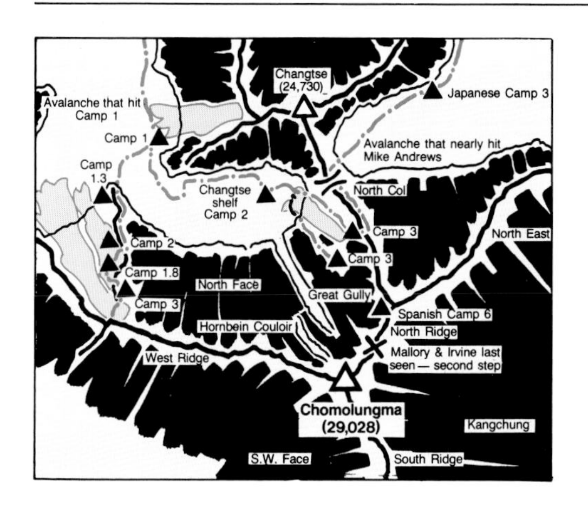

One of the most satisfying aspects of mountaineering is simply the process of exercising sound judgement.

We had all been shaken by the avalanche of 10 September but Austin in particular wanted to reconsider the route and had called everyone to advance base camp for a meeting. He later recalled what was going through his mind at this time.

> *The avo and the subsequent half hour had been a peculiar time. By the end of the day I could not recall clearly the details. As usual during a crisis in the mountains both mind and body worked at a higher level. For instance the telescope had usually given me trouble both in focusing and in locating the correct field of view. During the crisis it seemed to locate camp three and focus quite automatically. The decisions, such as they were, came automatically, but they were rational.*
> *At the same time in the back of my mind were thoughts and memories which remain clearly. They did not impinge on the situation but merely provided a backdrop to the action. There were feelings of concern for four people who had become very dear to me. I recalled the death of my close friend Archie Simpson who had fallen as we descended the Haast ridge in 1972. Other sad memories, inevitable in a lifetime of mountaineering, flooded back.*
> *One of the more satisfying aspects of mountaineering is the process of exercising sound judgement. Paradoxically the most satisfactory feeling is that which comes after the decision to continue has been made. That commitment can be euphoric. I felt strongly that any decision about the future of this expedition should not be made by one person.*

The north face and its prominent feature — the icecliff-guarded Great Gully. It stands above a shadowed camp two, upwards of a vertical mile of sunlight.

No one was looking forward to the meeting but by midday on 12 September we were all gathered in the old cook tent. Austin had just arrived back from a quick dash down to base camp to ask Pine Tree if he had any objection to our changing route. Surprisingly he hadn't, so long as we didn't conflict with the Japs who had now replaced the Catalans on the north ridge. So Austin kicked off, telling us how his first objective was for everyone to get home in one piece, 'We've had two near misses. I didn't enjoy watching them dig at camp three, not knowing if they were digging for bodies. I think we should change routes.'

Bruce looked very unhappy about the change of direction but for once was surprisingly quiet. Hugh said that mountaineering was a dangerous game with high risks and we should forge on despite the avalanche danger. The rest of us were prepared to change routes if a safer one could be found. I was concerned that we were trying to make a decision without knowing what the options were so after about an hour or so I suggested that Toyota should go up and investigate the north face to the left of the Great Gully. Austin agreed that we should do this,

The meeting at which we decided to abandon the west ridge was a depressing and formal recognition that, with the mountain in a continuously dangerous condition, our journey to the summit would be an especially risky and uncertain affair.

so that afternoon we hurried to camp one in driving sleet, prepared our skis and loads, and went to bed half-hoping that the storm would let us have a sleep-in in the morning because it was Friday the 13th. But there was no such luck. My diary records, 'Who isn't just a bit superstitious in an environment like this?'

At 5 am sleet was still stippling the tent nylon. I stuck my head out expecting bad weather but winking through the mist were millions of stars. I crawled out reluctantly and clumped over to the kitchen to make breakfast. One primus went dutifully so I put a brew on it. The other was very reluctant to go and I decided it was out of gas. Sleepily I removed the cylinder and immediately knew I had made a serious mistake. A loud hissing noise showed that the tank was still quite full and in a moment the tent had filled with gas and exploded in a burst of intense flame. I threw the primus at the small opening in the door but missed and it was flung back into the tent hosing flame like a runaway flame thrower. It was a thoroughly singed and courageless shadow of my former self which finally gathered a morsel of wit and dived through the door-hole, falling like a retarded porpoise on to the frosty rocks outside. Remarkably the only damage apart from singed clothes and a hair manicure was another door in the tent and a chunk of skin

The north face of Chomolungma, all 9,000 feet of it, and on the left the North Col. Our second camp two was in the small basin beneath the Col. In the foreground is the bottom section of the west ridge. (Colin Monteath)

off my hand, where my headlong dive into the rocks had been broken. For me Friday the 13th had begun quite badly but the camp had been successfully roused from sleep.

An hour and a half later we were skinning off up the glacier. Except for Shaun we were now using the old but solid ex 'Ruapehu Rental' skis which weren't that fancy but as Austin said 'they were real cheap' and they were easier to use in the difficult snow conditions. We took a different route on the glacier from the one to the west spur. This time we followed a trough close under Changtse, which took us easily up through a small ice fall to a terrace on the upper glacier. Now we turned left away from the north face and climbed steeply up towards the south face of Changtse. Blocks of avalanche debris showed it was no place to be after a storm but at the moment it was reasonably safe, except that by now the sun was high in the sky and the heat was becoming unbearable. By the time we reached the Changtse shelf at about 21,000 feet we were stripped down to the barest essentials of clothing and beginning to suffer. Shaun was going particularly well and was a hundred yards in front with Ross and Rob bringing up the rear. I waited on a small crest totally impressed by the surroundings. My eye couldn't help straying

Team Toyota wilting in the hothouse that was our second camp two. In the extreme climate of this camp, sleeping bags were a continuous necessity — when we weren't in them trying to keep warm, they were draped over the tents keeping us cool. (Rob Blackburne)

to the slopes a few hundred yards away below the Hornbein Couloir where the bodies of the Australians, Craig Nottle and Fred From, lay. It was a sobering thought.

Looking down the Rongbuk I was satisfied to see that we were already as high as Pukerua and the effort had been minimal, or at least would have been if it had been a bit cooler. By the time Ross and Rob arrived it was clear that Ross was becoming quite distressed by the heat, so I shouted ahead to Shaun to find the first safe camp spot. This he did in the lee of a great crevasse which should have stopped even the biggest avalanche, and then he generously skied down and took Ross's load. By the time we reached the campsite the heat had us gasping and we moved with the grace and speed of stunned mullets. Weakly we built a little lean-to shelter for Ross and then began to pitch the tents. 'Oh no!' we had brought no poles for one of them, so had to rig up a Heath Robinson frame with our skis. Meanwhile Shaun had taken out his thermometer. It already read 40°C but within moments the mercury shot up to the top of the scale at 50°C. Shaun extended the scale to the top of the glass and the mercury soon hit 55°C.

'My god, I don't think people can survive over 55 degrees,' I gasped. But they were going to have to; it continued to rise to the top of the glass to an estimated 62°C. By now we were stretched out on our backs in the tent, with Ross looking as if he were at death's door. At one stage as he flopped one arm down by his side he yelped in pain, 'Shit, I've burned myself on my zip!' An hour later, a cloud came over and it began to snow.

In the morning it was still snowing gently but at 10.30 am it cleared, so we climbed up to the crest above the camp to scrutinise the north face. To the left were the easy but evil-looking snow slopes that Shipton and Tilman had used to reach the North Col in 1938. Right of this rose the vast slopes of the north face. The main feature was the Great Gully which fell in a broad straight line from the summit 8,000 feet to the upper Rongbuk glacier. Four hundred yards to the right was the deep jagged line of the Hornbein Couloir and of course to the right of this the west ridge with its steep final 4,000 feet and its long level ridge leading to our old friend the west spur.

With smug satisfaction we watched a number of avalanches come off the west ridge. One went straight down the Japanese direct route with terrifying speed and we made jokes about Hasegawa fending off, side-stepping and so on. Another avalanche came down the Great Gully and billowed out over the Australian spur: 'That would have given the Australians a hurry-up' grinned Ross. But the north face to the left of the Great Gully was happily quiet and we were satisfied that a good route lay to the end of the Changtse shelf, and then up steepish snow slopes to a band of rock cliffs where it should be possible to traverse right into the Gully. We would then climb straight up to a point a few hundred feet from the top where a traverse line led up to the west ridge 150 feet from the summit. Simple as that. We clipped on our skis and enjoyed an exquisite run, 2,400 feet and about 3 miles back to camp one.

It now became clear that our new route offered a much shorter and quicker way to the top and we all began turning our minds to the crunch questions, who and when? Austin's plan was for Team Comalco to establish camp three at about

23,500 feet. Team Toyota would then supply this and Team Fairydown would go through to establish camp four in the Great Gully. This was the least desirable job because it meant that they would probably be too wiped out by the effort to make a summit attempt. Team Comalco would then go through, make a light assault camp at about 27,000 feet and go on to the top. The second attempt would be Toyota's. All we needed was a long settled period. About ten days would do nicely.

Over the next few days it snowed continuously. While Mike Andrews and Bruce were in camp two a big avalanche came down from somewhere in the mist and the blast broke the poles on one of their tents. They retreated to camp one where in the evening everyone was sitting about brewing in the Potala. Dick poked his head out to see where one roar, bigger than any other, was coming from and with well-disguised hysteria said, 'I think we'd better start running.' As a man, six bodies went through the small door-hole without touching the sides and began running down the valley. The huge powder avalanche fell down the almost vertical west face of Changtse and roared out towards camp one. By the time the blast hit, six bodies lay behind rocks holding on for dear life.

A few miles away, just below the North Col, four of the Japanese team were descending to their camp three when a large slab avalanche buried them. One man died. The margin between success and failure, life and death, is very fine on high climbs in the Himalaya.

The weather continued bad for several days and much new snow fell. Team Toyota descended to base camp where Austin put the latest plan to the resting Fairydown team. They were a bit upset that they were to be the sacrificial lambs, putting in camp four. After much discussion they opted to try to put in a camp five as well so that they could have a crack at the top. Having spent an hour or so coming to a decision on this they then embarked on a topic that evoked much greater passion: whether Warwick in his newspaper articles and Austin in his radio tapes should tell the whole truth at the risk of upsetting loved ones? In particular, should Mike Perry's name be used in despatches about the avalanche at camp three at the risk of worrying his family in Christchurch? The argument raged back and forth but finally Mike asked that his name be removed from both the article and the tape. The ever-patient Austin went through his tape carefully, leaving a blank wherever Mike's name had been used. Then Rheinberger served an appalling meal of lentils, peppers and garlic — the effects were instantaneous and not very nice.

I was beginning to sense that our chances of getting to the top were becoming slimmer by the day and in a moment of weakness had decided to use oxygen. Shaun and I even carried bottles, masks and regulators to camp one but the weight was ridiculous. We would have had to carry an extra 20 pounds on top of all our other equipment to nearly 27,000 feet before turning the oxygen on, as the full tank would last no more than six hours.

Camp one was a cold and bleak transit station. Our comfortable belief that it was a haven from avalanches was abruptly shattered on 15 September when a massive powder avalanche rolled down off Changtse. The blast all but destroyed the Potala — our mess tent.

By 20 September the weather had cleared again. The plan was for Teams Comalco and Toyota to carry loads to camp two, and then to jointly establish camp three. Shaun decided he'd carry a light load to camp two, and then return to camp one. He said he would join us later. At 6 am while it was still dark the Comalco boys skied off up the glacier and we decided to have another brew before leaving. In the Potala I asked Shaun why he had decided to adopt a different plan to ours. He said he preferred to carry two light loads rather than one big one, and his plan left more time for the new snow to compact. It made such good sense that we all decided to do it that way and in a few minutes we had thrown our sleeping bags out of our packs and were following Comalco up the glacier. Behind us a spectacular dawn light had turned Pumori and Cho Oyu a brilliant gold, and a perfectly sinister cigar-shaped cloud had formed over Chomolungma.

As we approached the Changtse shelf we were startled by an unusual sound. Was it some kind of avalanche? No. Was it a giant bird? No, it sounded much more like a runaway express train. We peered into the post-dawn gloom, searching the slopes above for the danger. And then over the crest appeared Mike Andrews, skiing for all he was worth. The style was that of a self-taught Taranaki mountaineering machine, not pretty but effective. The most curious thing was

From advance base camp, Chomolungma, with its storm cap. Let it rip, jetstream!

the noise he made as he turned, a cross between a Russian weightlifter and a steam train. Mike had carried his load up to the shelf and couldn't resist a run down, before climbing back up and carrying on to camp two.

We arrived at the camp just behind Steve, Dick and Bruce and announced our change of plan. It was as if we'd said the rest of the expedition had just been wiped out. There was an electric silence followed by an outburst from Bruce. He felt we had really let them down. We couldn't understand this as the only difference was that we would be going to camp three a day later than planned. It seemed strange how we would constantly acknowledge the need for good judgement and personal initiative, but then when someone showed these qualities others tried to make them feel as if they had just done something despicable. A little disappointed we skied back to camp one.

Next morning we were back again in time to see Comalco making good progress up the vast snow face of the lower north face. By midday as usual the sun was scorching down and avalanches began to pour off Changtse. Once the sun hit Comalco their progress slowed to a crawl. Steve Bruce recorded

---

Steve Bruce and Bruce Farmer skin along the Changtse shelf towards camp two. Early-morning trips to camp two were a constant race against the arrival of the sun. Before sunrise, heavy clothing, maybe even a down suit, was appropriate, but when the sun appeared over the north ridge the temperature soared to about 30°C and anyone unfortunate enough to be caught on the shelf was roasted. (Mike Andrews)

---

their progress.

> *The powder seems to be on top of a hard base and at an angle conducive to sliding off. I'm not happy with the conditions. I wait beside a small rocky outcrop while Hugh and Mike plug on. Once they have tested the slope I follow.*
> *Everyone takes a turn digging the trench for the others to follow in the deep snow. The weather begins to pack in. Whiteout conditions. We reach the point which we had been aiming for and which we had picked out from below as being where the camp should be located. Reality is a sweeping snow slope. There are a couple of rock patches but none appears to offer the possibility of a safe campsite. We want protection from the only too real danger of the camp being avalanched off the mountain.*
> *Bruce is going particularly strongly. The rest of us look shot. Grimly we follow him into the cloud.*
> *Finally I announce a mutiny — we are going no higher in the hope of finding a site for the camp. I think I could have kept on going but I ran out of motivation. Dick finds the spot to stash the gear by excavating snow beneath an overhanging rock.*

At about 3 pm we were relieved to see Comalco get safely back to the upper glacier and then, with various levels of competence, ski back to the camp. They arrived one by one, looking knackered but happy with a good day's work. Bruce Farmer was the last to arrive. He had hardly ever been on skis before and Chomolungma would seem to be a rather extreme place to learn, but Bruce is nothing if not different. He arrived at the camp covered in snow from head to foot as if he had tunnelled down, and for once the noisy optimism was missing but beneath his wide-brimmed fashionable Chinese sun hat he was sporting a wide grin. We all chattered enthusiastically over a brew, then one by one they skied away towards camp one. All hard feelings about the previous day's confrontation were thankfully gone.

The brief notes in my diary for 23 September sum the day up pretty well: 'Sleepless night — calm, cold. Brew at 4 am. Away 5.30 am with heavy loads. End of ski tracks 6.45 am. Begin climbing, cursing people who come down steps [breaking them and making them useless]. Very hard work. Reach the fixed rope through the rock band — 50 feet of probably the only real climbing on the entire route. We climb changeable snow straight up, dangerous as a sleeping tiger. Reach gear dumped by Comalco at about midday. Ross knackered — says he won't come up here again, too much pain. We all encourage him [not to make a decision on that until much later].'

We cut and stamped out a ledge and surveyed the situation while eating some lunch. Our position at about 23,600 feet appeared to be the only possible site for camp three as, with some excavation, the small rock step would protect the tent a little. There were no other such places within sight, just countless acres of desperately unstable snow. About 250 yards of the stuff separated us from the

Great Gully, so close but yet so far in the prevailing conditions. To précis our situation, up looked awful but down looked worse. The frustrating thing was that nowhere was there any difficulty. It was just bloody dangerous. Pierre Beghin had said 'the problem with Everest is that the walk-in ends at 8,000 metres [26,000 feet].'

We shouted some friendly messages at the Japanese way below us on the North Col and then began excavating the ledge. Unfortunately before it was big enough we hit rock. We pitched two tents and I banged in a couple of pegs, clipped a rope to them and passed it right through the tent that Rob and I were in, and then passed the end of the rope to Ross and Shaun in the other tent. Rob and I chuckled as we heard Shaun say to Ross, 'If you hear anything coming, grab this.' We made noises like avalanches and laughed some more. In the middle of the afternoon the avalanches began to pour off Changtse and across the shelf. Then to our utter astonishment we saw Team Fairydown climbing slowly up towards the shelf. 'The bastards must be crazy,' breathed Ross. It was much too late to be where they were and we all yelled a pathetic warning, 'Go home ... avalanches.' The Japanese on the North Col probably thought we were yelling at them. To reinforce the point an absolute 'motha' roared down, completely covering 200 yards of the shelf. Fairydown got the message and turned for home. Two hours later it began to snow heavily and this continued throughout the night. What more snow would do to the already unstable slope did not bear thinking about.

By dawn it had stopped snowing but an ominously heavy sky gave promise of more. At 8.30 am I shouldered my load and started upwards, attempting to cross to the Great Gully by hugging the base of the rockband that ran diagonally across from the camp. Fifty desperate steps in thigh-deep snow and I realised that that line of approach was hopeless and returned to the tents. Then without loads, Ross, Rob and I set out again, this time climbing straight up where a thin layer of snow and ice covered a band of steeper rock. Shaun was feeling awful so stayed in his tent. The new line was an unexpected delight and we cramponed quickly up several hundred feet of steep ground. As we climbed, the atmosphere of impending storm grew more and more heavy, but I was keen to find a safe route into the Great Gully before we descended.

As I climbed towards a probable viewpoint Rob called out to me, 'I think we'd better get down, Ding, I don't think the storm is far away.'

'Hang on, I think we'll get a good view from up here,' I called back to him. I made one final fast burst and reached the knob, feeling very satisfied that here at 24,000 feet I could still move quickly. Ross and Rob joined me and we surveyed the scene. From the knob a traverse line appeared to climb diagonally across into the Great Gully. The continuation straight up to the north ridge also looked good in these conditions (a new route for someone some day).

Happy that a safe route existed we hurried down to the tents, sending off little surface avalanches as we went. By the time we reached the tents we were gripped by a great urgency to get down before the storm struck. We packed quickly and began down the horrible slope, wondering what made it all hang together. Halfway down Shaun said, 'I know people who'd pay hundreds, no, thousands

to ski snow like this.'

'Yeah, and I know someone who'd pay thousands to get off it,' I retorted.

By the time we reached our skis visibility was down to a few feet and it was snowing heavily. We hurried to get away from beneath the face. The ski-run home was the worst of the trip. A wind crust had formed on the new snow and made it impossible to turn. I decided the best conditions might be on the face of Changtse where avalanches had consolidated the slopes, and so I skied vaguely in that direction without the luxury of visibility. Suddenly my heart missed a beat as I realised that I had skied off the top of a 20-foot-high bank and was flying. In the moments before impact I saw below me blocks of avalanche debris as big as sacks of potatoes and then I was amongst them. My dear old 'Ruapehu Rentals' were buried up to the hilt and the only way I could extricate myself was to get out of the bindings. Remarkably neither skis nor body were at all damaged but all desire to ski the slopes of Changtse had gone. I pulled out my skis like an aberrant spear thrower and soberly skied back to camp two.

As we departed for camp one the Fairydown boys arrived, loaded like mules. At the end of the shelf we met a sweaty Perry labouring up in the heat, cameras

After retreating from the blast-furnace heat and avalanches of the Changtse shelf, Team Fairydown recuperate in the cool of the evening at camp one.

and a radio swinging like strange metronomes in front of him.

'What the hell have you got in that pack,' we greeted him.

'I've taken out everything except essentials. This is virtually just personal stuff I'm taking to the summit, weighs about 50 bloody pounds.'

'Shit. We're taking nothing but what we can fit in our pockets.'

Safely back in the Potala we sorted through the mail like starved beasts. As usual seven for Cullen, three for Norman and a sackful for Rob. For me there was still no mail from my wife, Corrina, so I talked to Austin about doing a quick trip out to Xegar Post Office to see what I could find. His reaction was a true measure of his sensitivity and skill as a leader. He knew we were reaching a crucial point but he knew that unless I resolved my immediate problem I'd be useless on the hill anyway. Rob was keen to come out with me, so like a couple of kids leaving school for the holidays we hurried down to base camp. As we went we felt as if we were descending from winter to spring. Temperatures had plummetted on

Just before camp two, on the Changtse shelf, we had to cross a couple of hundred yards of avalanche debris. The avalanche, which had deposited this debris, occurred while Team Fairydown paused, mist-bound, a hundred yards beneath. The fear of avalanches became almost tolerable in the daytime, but mist would set the nerves jangling, and at night deep horror of burial and suffocation ran rampant. It became 'de rigueur' to wear a Pieps (a radio transmitter and receiver which transmits beeps at regular intervals and can pick them up) while sleeping and common to dangle a knife from the ceiling of one's tent in case of burial. (Shaun Norman)

the mountain over the last couple of weeks. Snow covered the moraine almost to advance base camp and the little green basin was frosty and cold. The stream had frozen up and the lake had shrunk to an icy puddle surrounded by cracked mud. At the East Rongbuk the river was no longer a churning brown torrent and we hopped easily across rocks, which was lucky because the yak herders had stolen the rope. At base camp Pine Tree and Mr Chan greeted us happily, they knew they would soon be going home.

We set off before dawn next day and to begin with it seemed that Mr Chan's driving had improved while he had been at base camp, but once we crossed the high pass I realised it was just an illusion created by the relative comfort of the Toyota. His habit of free-wheeling down hill and breaking only to save our lives had, if anything, got worse. Much later when my nerves couldn't stand it any longer I encouraged him to stop on the pretext of needing a leak. I then eased him out of the driver's seat and into the back, and I got behind the wheel and demonstrated that it was possible to go down hill in control. He was very polite and grateful but it made absolutely no difference: on the next hill he hurtled downwards, braking only for the hairpins.

If descending to base camp was like passing into spring, down in the lower valley was like being on another planet. The sun shone warmly on a world of golden barley, in the fields happy people were harvesting for all they were worth. After the stark world of Chomolungma we felt reborn.

At Xegar there was no mail so we decided to go on to Xigatse in the forlorn hope that we might be able to phone New Zealand. Apart from my own desire to hear from Corrina, Austin was of course very keen to hear from Julie about the birth of their child and had given us a Melbourne number to phone. Rob had a ladyfriend to call and Shaun wanted us to phone his mum in London.

At Xigatse a new tourist hotel had opened in our absence, so feeling very dirty and unkempt we snuck into the place like burglars and were soon being shown to rooms with lush eiderdowns, showers and digital phones. Sadly, the eiderdowns were the only things that worked. Many hours of calling and even three new phones produced nothing except a few laughs: I began to wonder was there some truth in the schoolboy joke that there are no phones in China because there are so many Wings and Wongs people would always wing the wong number. We did, however, become very practised at saying *neehow* (hello) to the operator. In the last days of the expedition this was to become our catch word.

I would recommend this kind of break from a mountain to anyone on a long expedition because next day we returned to base camp feeling thoroughly refreshed and ready for the last push. Both Rob and I were confident that in a week we would be on top.

In the meantime only Rheinberger and Warwick had been to camp three and bad weather had prevented them from pushing any further. Peter Allen had

Mike Rheinberger heading for camp three on the north face. These slopes stretched upwards for more than 3,000 feet before reaching the Yellow Band, a short, steepish rock barrier which offered the only difficulties on the entire route.

been forced to come down with an abscessed tooth which Rob removed as soon as we got back, and Mike Perry had decided that conditions were too dangerous, an opinion later endorsed by Warwick and Rheinberger who said the slope 'settled and cracked' as they descended.

On 27 September we climbed quickly to advance base camp with a feeling that this was it: we would get up within the next week or miss out. Comalco were to keep two days ahead of us and so they moved up to camp two. Once there, Mike Andrews went for a walk to 'recce' the slopes to the left of our present route to camp three. His enquiry was answered by an enormous roar and those at camp two watched in horror as a great avalanche began down from between the North Col and camp three. Mike ran for his skis, reached them and considered putting them on for a moment but realised there wasn't time. He bundled them under his arm and began to run. Suddenly he started his own avalanche and was carried out of sight. The big avalanche piled debris along the base of the Changtse face to his right but happily he was able to extricate himself from his own slide, clip on his skis and return to camp. Comalco, however, were all badly shaken by the experience and returned to camp one to await better conditions.

The 28th was a grey stormy day and Austin came down to advance base camp to discuss another new plan. The conclusion was for two teams, Comalco and Toyota, to keep at the north face while a new team had a go at the north ridge. With so little time left this was a way of spreading the odds. Sadly, Shaun was taken from Toyota and replaced by Rheinberger. We liked Rheinberger, even the jokes he told — after two months he was still capable of telling a new one every day — but suddenly we realised how close we had all become in Toyota. The north ridgers were Dick, Shaun, Mike Perry, Peter Allen and Warwick.

To relieve the tension of the day, in the late afternoon we launched into an insane game of colonial cricket, New Zealand versus the rest of the world. The wicket was an old surveyor's tripod (probably a priceless memento of Mallory's last expedition), the bat was several glacier wands taped together and the ball was a rock tied inside a sock. It was probably the highest game of cricket ever played, with most of us lumbering about in down suits, partly as protection against a blow from the ball and partly against the biting cold. With New Zealand leading 20 to 19, Warwick came in as the last batsman for the rest of the world. White-faced and crash helmet askew he bravely faced Norman bowling — body liners from 20 feet! Warwick didn't see the first two balls, which narrowly missed the wicket and raised excitement to near hysteria level. The next ball he hit well. Three balls later he nicked one into slips to take the series. Everyone, winners and losers, went quite mad, whacking Warwick on the back and forming an arch of honour for his return to the pavilion. The injury list was impressive: one severely bruised genitals, one chipped ankle bone, one broken thumbnail, five minor body bruises, two strained bowling arms, two cracked heads (caused by a collision taking a catch).

The last ball of a highly successful world series. Warwick Anderson behind the bat, as Shaun Norman sends the rock in the sock down at a fearful speed.

Diary: 29 September. Comalco go to camp two and the north ridge team moves to one. Toyota waits at A.B.C. [advance base camp] and Austin goes down to try to find something out about his new family. 30 September. Weather clear but a huge wind plume off Chomolungma. Comalco wait at camp two and the north ridgers move up to join them. Austin arrives back from Xegar with no news.
1 October. Today we move up for the last time. Comalco went to camp three this morning. Including today we have got twelve days to get up and down again — the truck leaves at dawn on 13 October. The minimum time we could do it in is seven days return to base camp, so of course there is a chance that given fine weather and good conditions, on the evening of the 7th we could be back in base camp celebrating our highest ambition. It's hard to believe that we've worked all these years and the outcome now rests on a few lucky days — the throw of a dice! We have of course risked much to reach our present

Dick Price puts a Chinese kite through its paces on Chomolungma. Dick's kite-flying friends in Oamaru will never get their kites to 19,000 feet.

tenuous position and there will be much more risk, at least two days of critical risk — the summit day and getting down. At the beginning of this trip I interviewed a number of key expedition members and one of the questions I asked was, 'How high do you think is the risk of a serious accident?' All answered 'very high', one said as high as one in three. Sobering stuff!

I was writing the above entry as Rob went to do the radio sched. He came back fifteen minutes later looking grim.

'Guess what's happened,' he said as he came into the cook tent.

'Another avo,' said Ross with a bored tone.

'Where?'

'Just to the right of camp three. Comalco didn't see. They were in their tents but according to Pete Allen who was watching from camp two it was bigger than the one that just about got Mike Andrews. It's taken out most of the line of steps

---

Mike Rheinberger at the heart of our radio system. An expedition like ours with small groups operating out of contact with each other was highly dependent on radio communication.

up to camp three.' We were all so bloody tired of avalanches.

It was snowing heavily as Austin, Rheinberger, Ross, Rob and I tramped up to camp one in the afternoon. We were worried about Comalco. On the 8 pm sched Bruce told of their intention to push on in the morning. Austin told him to feel no pressure from the rest of the expedition to push it. He finished, 'It's my preference that you come down.' By the time we crawled into our sleeping bags it had stopped snowing and the moon shone with a weak light on the Rongbuk but small flakes of snow still floated around in the air. In camp three Steve Bruce recorded his feelings.

> *Van Noorden rationalises that the snow is not too bad and should get better higher up (a theory that I subscribe to given the amount of snow which is being blown off the mountain higher up, the moot point however being exactly how high you have to survive to reach the good conditions). Mike Andrews offers no hope as he states that he is just 'keen to keep on with it.' I just feel scared. If I back out of it and head down I am labelled 'the one that let the side down' and cost them the summit. On the other hand I know that to follow the death and glory boys 'lemming-like' is possibly even more of a no-win situation. In fact to do so could be a total loss situation! I sleep little. I think back to New Zealand and the last time I said 'what the hell' and against my instincts went for it. On that occasion I triggered a massive slab avalanche which took me 500 feet or so down a steep slope half burying me. I was lucky and managed to keep on top of the main avalanche. Tomorrow I might not be so lucky. There is a heavy snow fall during the night.*

At 5.30 am we schedded again with Comalco and the north ridgers. Bruce was having trouble deciding whether to go on or come down; both Mike and Steve weren't feeling well. By 9 am Steve had decided to come down and on the radio Austin asked those at camp two to watch him. 'If necessary dig him out at the bottom. ... I've grown quite fond of him,' he finished with a grin. By 10 am Mike Andrews had also decided to descend. Bruce and Hugh were talking about carrying on.

'Bugger. I don't want to have to go to Rosemary and tell her that Bruce won't be coming back,' said Austin. By 1 pm Bruce was sounding more confused than ever: torn between going up and down but knowing in his heart that there wasn't a chance of up and just plain not wanting to admit defeat. By now Steve and Mike had flagged the descent away and had returned to their sleeping bags.

Meanwhile the north ridgers were still watching and waiting at camp two. At camp one we too were frustrated but threw ourselves enthusiastically into endless brews and a game of five hundred.

Steve Bruce records the night of 2 October and the dawning of 3 October thus:

> *Developed a headache during the night. It was a clear night but very*

blustery. Spindrift pouring down the mountain in unbelievable quantities. Woke from a fitful sleep to find the tent completely covered in a cocoon of snow. Took quite a while to dig even part of the door out to allow air to enter. Spindrift was filling the space I cleared as quickly as I was able to clear it! Spent the remainder of the night keeping the air space clear, working at half-hourly intervals with Hugh. The night ended at 4 am when Hugh lit the primus and announced that it was a great morning outside and that we should stop mucking about and start getting ready to climb. The view out the door of the tent tells another story — the spindrift is blowing like water down the slope. My headache got worse and I subsequently threw up in the entrance to the tent. Hugh was sufficiently sympathetic to hand me a billy and suggest I clean the mess up.

At 5.30 am we turned on the radio at camp one. Dick came in from camp two saying it was too windy to move. Then a subdued-sounding Bruce said that Mike and Steve had been vomiting all night and, although Steve was coming down, Mike would continue up with Hugh and himself. Austin asked Dick for a medical

A small but well-known piece of Nepal, Mt Nuptse (25,851 feet), seen through the Lho La from base camp.

opinion on Mike. 'Mike has a history of nausea at around 24,000 feet, but he should know what's best for himself,' said Dick thoughtfully. Five minutes later Mike decided to come down. Bruce and Hugh would go on.

At 9 am Austin left for advance base camp to fetch some food and fresh radio batteries. Ross carried a load down, Rheinbuggles went back to bed and Rob and I set off on skis for the Lho La. We took the telescope with us to watch progress on the north face. Conscious of the avalanche danger we kept away from the west spur and skied up close under Khumbutse. Only thirty minutes from camp we reached the crest of the symmetrical pass and were able to look into the familiar country of the Khumbu. The almost friendly shapes of Ama Dablam, Taweche and Cholatse were etched across the distant skyline. 'If we really went for it, we could be into some of that Sherpa grog tonight,' I grinned, feeling my non-drinking vow beginning to wear thin. Closer to us the rugged bulk of Nuptse looked steep but inviting. Below us the Khumbu ice fall tumbled in a chaos of ice blocks from the Western Cwm. We could clearly see the Indian advance base camp at the top of the ice fall. In a few days, five of that expedition would be dead — one killed in a fall, the rest from exposure and exhaustion.

A gale made it unpleasant to loiter so we were soon sliding silently back down the glacier, again keeping away from the threat of the west spur. We were almost out on to the Rongbuk glacier when a muffled roar turned our heads. From the west spur a big avalanche slid with amazing speed down and out on to the glacier. 'A two-minute miss on this trip is not even close,' we grinned at each other.

In the middle of the Rongbuk we set up the telescope and focused on the north face. Immediately we could see that things up there were incredibly unpleasant. Where we were the day was calm and warm but the entire north face was being whipped by a gale into a maelstrom of blown snow. Trying to locate any humanity in that mad world was like trying to locate someone in a storm at sea. The snow was blowing in thick eddies which moved in every direction including up the slope. Eventually we did locate tiny black dots of humanity in that seething mass of white, not two but four. It was like an illustration from *The Worst Journey in the World* where wild-looking men, reduced to the level of hunted animals, battle hunched against the storm while geysers of snow erupt all around them. We could identify Mike Andrews looking sick and confused and being shepherded down by Bruce. Hugh and Steve were going much better. We packed the telescope and skied back to camp to catch the one o'clock sched. It contained nothing of importance so we settled down to more brews and more games of five hundred.

At 4 pm Rob turned on the radio. He was winning at cards and was in a mad mood so he squeaked into the set, 'Neehow, Mrs Norman, this is the Chinese Authorities.' His discourse was cut short by the stern voice of Doctor Dick. 'Dick Price here Rob. This is very serious. Please repeat after me. Mike Andrews has

---

Mind still clouded from the onset of cerebral oedema, Mike Andrews discovers he has frost-bite. Incredibly, four days later, accompanied by Rob Blackburne he reached Burwood Hospital in Christchurch, New Zealand.

frost-bite. The skin of his fingertips is quite frozen and a whitish-grey colour. The fingers are being thawed. ...' A sobered Rob repeated the message. 'We are bringing him down to one and want the following gear ready: oxygen, sleeping mask, narcain, heparin, the French injectables, some needles.'

Later Hugh described how just as they left camp three, the remaining tent could not stand the weight of snow on it any longer and gracefully collapsed into an icy grave.

The heat that tormented us in the upper glacier was mercurial. A quiet breeze could slash the temperature, and the wind-storm on the morning of the abandonment of camp three (north face), in fact, yielded our lowest temperatures. Peter Allen, Dick Price and Warwick Anderson anxiously witness the end of camp three.

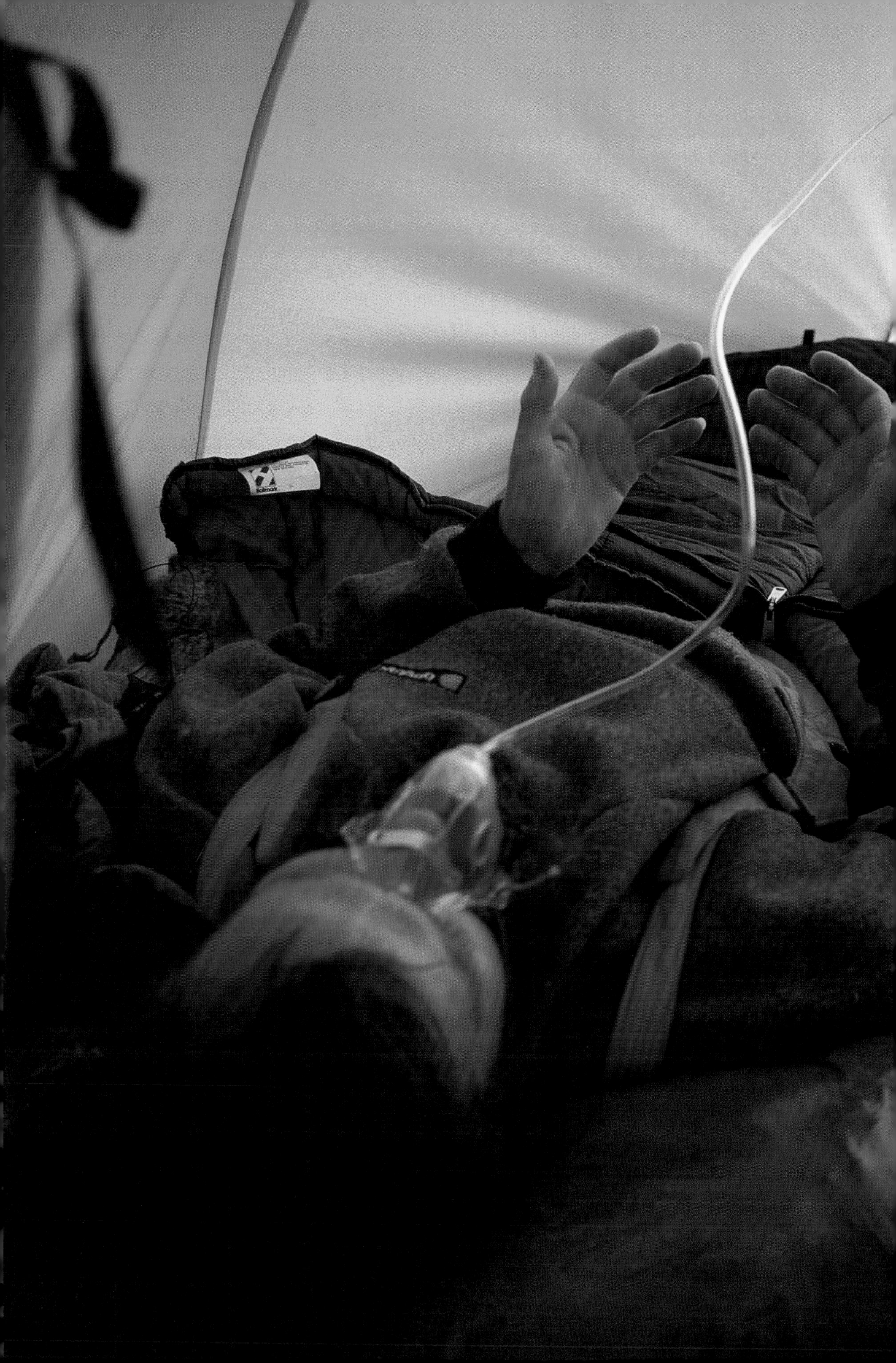

Chapter 8 The North Ridge

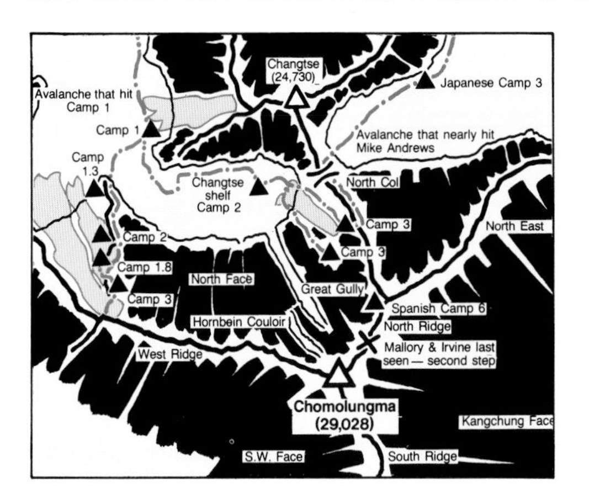

I remember being a double mixture of hot and cold at this time — hot body, cold hands, hot ambition and somewhat colder fear.

With what remained at camp three buried by snow, the unsettled weather and only a week left it was clear even to an incurable optimist like Bruce Farmer that our bid for the north face had failed. The only chance, and it was an incredibly long shot, was a fast lightweight push on the north ridge. Over the next few days Mike Andrews left the mountain for urgent medical attention in New Zealand and Rob selflessly volunteered to accompany him as nurse; Steve Bruce was brought down with a variety of serious medical problems which put him on an intravenous drip for two days, and Dick and Peter stayed at camp one to look after Steve; the rest of us installed ourselves in camp two for the last ditch attempt. Meanwhile a telegram had arrived for Austin. He kept it until a quiet moment presented itself when he could indulge himself in the news of Julie and their new child. Finally his nervous fingers took the message from its envelope. It read 'Your 4,000 yuan transferred from our Hong Kong branch to Peking branch today.'

At camp two, Ross, Mike Perry and I had taken a good look at the slopes up on to the north ridge and decided that they were too dangerous in their present condition. I felt that the risk might have been justifiable if there had been a chance of getting to the top but not otherwise. While Bruce, Hugh, Rheinberger, Shaun and Warwick went for the north ridge, the rest of us would carry down the essentials from camp two and camp one. Dick was also keen to go for the north ridge but was torn between his commitment to treating Steve and his mountaineering ambition. Finally on the 4.30 am sched on 6 October he explained he couldn't come as Steve's condition wasn't stable — he hadn't urinated for forty-eight hours.

Mike Andrews receiving comprehensive medical treatment at camp one. Dick Price administered oxygen and drugs to open the circulation and thin the blood, but already an ominous demarcation between damaged and undamaged flesh is visible. (Ross Cullen)

There followed one of the funniest departures since Dunkirk. To begin with poor old Rheinberger was thrown into a total quandary because Dick had been going to bring up with him the long-awaited letter from the girlfriend. 'Yes or no?': no one was quite sure what the question had been but Rheinberger wasn't going up until he had the answer. He asked Dick to read the letter out to him over the radio, and then he tramped 20 yards from the camp with the radio to a relatively private place. Everyone strained their ears. Horrors! The radio wouldn't work. (Mills and Boon could be interested in this one.) The radio was swapped and the letter painfully flowed. The answer was not yes or no, but it seemed to be good news to Mike, and he returned to the camp ready to do battle with the north ridge.

After about an hour Hugh and Warwick had enough hot water for a brew. It was a help yourself affair but no one seemed to be able to find any ingredients to put in the water. As I listened from the depths of my sleeping bag to the sound of people crashing about trying to find something for breakfast or some piece of errant equipment, I was quite happy that I wasn't going. In the freezing darkness of pre-dawn, muesli and fetid brews were swallowed without enjoyment, it was just fuel that needed to be consumed for use later. Then the still air was rent by

Shaun Norman studying the sunset on the north face. (Hugh Van Noorden)

a dreadful obscenity. Bruce's lamp had failed. Ross lent him his. Then there was another outburst as Warwick ran out of toilet paper. An angry exchange took place between Hugh and me as he ripped open our tent door and demanded toilet paper. Now worse happened, Bruce heaved up his enormous load and tore the shoulder strap out of his pack. He tried to fix it with wire but finally admitted defeat and took mine. Warwick went off to use the toilet paper and while he was away everyone else set off with cheery good wishes from Ross, Mike and me. When Warwick returned he had frozen fingers and had to spend thirty minutes thawing them out in hot water. Warwick takes up the story from there.

A cold wind was blowing but stars winked in the darkness promising a fine day — a cloudless one in fact. Each person moved along under the weight of his pack and of his thoughts, plodding initially in the direction of the bergschrund under the North Col, pretty well following the first sixty minutes or so of our north face route.
The sun meanwhile hit the summit above, turning the bleakness of pre-

Mike Rheinberger on the arete leading to the north ridge while below, Bruce Farmer, Shaun Norman and Warwick Anderson leave the couloir. The dot above Mike Rheinberger's pack is camp two. (Hugh Van Noorden)

dawn to rosy pink, to brown-yellow, to the rock and ice glitter of full day. Climbers and sunshine met just before the schrund. From there it was going to be a much warmer experience. I remember being a double mixture of hot and cold at this time — hot body, cold hands, hot ambition and somewhat colder fear — for now we were in the firing line of one of the prospective routes we had considered: a fast hike up the avalanche couloir that had disgorged its all on Mike Andrews' rapidly fleeing footsteps a week earlier and prior to the last snowstorm. Assuming no fresh avalanche monsters lurked there, it would be a rapid and easy access route to relatively high on the north ridge. The other possible line began from the same point at the schrund, another couloir promising shorter and more direct access to the North Col itself.

Hugh plugged a few steps on the start to the latter couloir and said its snow was suspect so Shaun, Bruce and I rested at the schrund while he and Mike checked out the avalanche couloir. It was hard to know what it would be like in its upper reaches but the lower section looked all right. Clearly it had been swept clean in the fairly recent past. The pair made rapid progress into black figurine distance while we waited — Shaun and I in the bunker protection of the crevasse, Bruce outside with an eye on the others' fortunes. We thought they would try to break out of the long couloir to the ridge in favour of the couloir leading to the Col since this, to me anyway, seemed to be the more promising prospect, the upper reaches of the long couloir being doubtful territory. Several times it looked as if they would break out left on to the line of the other, only to move back into the centre of the long couloir. Just before the pair did climb out to the left, the three of us made a double check of the Col-direct prospect. It looked promising in a doubtful fashion and Shaun commented that the deepish snow we were standing in was actually quite stable. Further up, however, the Col-direct couloir curved out of sight between what looked like loaded slopes. We decided to take the long line behind the others.

The trip up the couloir was tiring and tense. The surface was excellent, the gradient a forty-degree dream, the run-out potentially a never-ending one. Each climbed separately avoiding the fall-line of whoever was above. Mike and Hugh, who had probably done the same thing, appeared now to be sitting on a snow-bank ledge well up on the side, lunching and waiting. The break-out into the Col-direct couloir had not come about. When we got a little closer and looked across, we saw why: that nice, short route would have been an accessway to bland and rolling expanses of open avalanche slope with the emphasis on

Our last sunset on Chomolungma. During the night the first winter storm broke, battering the north ridge team and setting a beleaguered tone to our withdrawal from the lower camps.

readiness in the rolling department. And all of it deep. Instead, Mike and Hugh were now back on the move, on a line up an arete above their lunch stop. We stopped for lunch in the same place.

That was about the pace of the day. Mike and Hugh plugged steps up ahead, Bruce came third, followed by Shaun, followed by me. Good snow for step-plugging but a tiring slog under an overbearing sun. No fear, however, of avalanches, it was a good stable route. It was clear that the ridge would not be reached in the day. There was a good shelf for an encampment about 1,500 feet above us on our arete, so Graeme Dingle told us when we schedded at 1 pm. Down below, camp two was on its last tent poles.

By about 3.30 or 4 o'clock all five of us were at the shelf. Mike and Hugh had put up their very small tent on an excavated platform in the shelter of a moderate-sized rock. We erected our rather larger one on another shovelled-out niche about 30 feet below. I remember it taking some time to prepare the site as a very brisk wind was now blowing.

In early October the weather pattern changed from the all-too-familiar afternoon monsoon snow-cloud to a brooding storm sky, as seen here from camp two (north face). With typical caprice the full force of the storm held back until the north ridge team's hopes were building.

The poles were fitted into the sleeves and the dome put up. Considerable care was taken in anchoring the tent securely, and then it was strictly retirement within.

Meanwhile down at camp two, Perry, Cullen and I were well on the way with the depressing job of clearing the camp. There is little that is more depressing than having to carry down a load of stuff that you've really suffered to carry up, particularly when you are returning unsuccessful. We built a sled out of skis and loaded everything except food and a few odds and ends on to it, staggering about as the afternoon lassitude got to us and becoming more and more hot and bothered as the load on the sled began to rival Chomolungma itself. The ravens with a superb sense of timing arrived to clean up any food left behind. We made one little cache of food and a stove in case the north ridgers had to return that way, and then we turned to the task of moving the sled. We heaved and heaved, then sank down in the snow already out of breath.

'The bastard won't budge,' puffed Ross.

'Let's try again,' I encouraged, hoping that by some miracle the monster might

The north ridge team pitch camp on the arete. They spent two nights on the threshold of our by then predictable barrier at 24,000 feet. (Hugh Van Noorden)

take off down to camp two. We did succeed in pulling the thing a few feet but it pushed up a huge heap of snow in front of itself and stuck fast.

'A fucking snow plough,' said Mike in disgust. More depressed than ever we unloaded the equipment, dismantled the sled and built another. This time a smaller one with the runners in a triangular configuration. On to this we loaded about 120 pounds, the rest we heaved on to our backs, and at about 6 pm we set off feeling more like huskies at the South Pole than human beings.

Before long we ran into the first avalanche debris, and here our troubles began in earnest as we battled to move the beast through the snow blocks. Eventually we carried our packs through and then returned for the sled. Every time anything made a noise above us on the face of Changtse we looked up expecting to see an avalanche coming down on us. Once we had dragged and carried the sled through the debris, there was a swathe behind us as if a snow groomer had been through making a track for skiers.

At 8 pm, radio sched time, we had only reached the end of the Changtse shelf. It was almost dark, we were worn out and very grumpy. 'Dog team to any station listening,' we called into the radio. When the other stations responded, we began howling and yapping like three lunatics. This idiocy, however, soon restored some of our humour and in the gloom we continued down to the bottom of the ramp. By then it was pitch dark and we'd had enough, so we abandoned the sled and skied on down to camp one. It was exciting stuff in the dark! Next morning we returned and completed the job.

Happily Austin was able to sell camp one virtually intact to a man who happened into advance base camp and announced that he was a member of the 1986 Canadian West Ridge team. If that's not good business then I don't know what is. And it was good for the 'dog team' because it meant that we only had a few husky loads to take down to advance base camp. Meanwhile Steve had almost recovered and, a shadow of his former herculean self, was helping to carry down equipment from advance base camp.

Warwick continues the story of the 'north ridgers':

> *It was at first unclear just how far this new camp three (the expedition's third) was from the north ridge. It was thought to be perhaps as much as a thousand feet. This concept was thrown out when a Japanese climber was seen descending. In the wind and in the cold he neither saw nor heard whoever had spotted him but he was very close. It would take in the vicinity of half an hour to crest out in the morning.*
> *This was not to be. The wind strengthened and cloud came in. The sched that evening brought a prediction of deteriorating weather as observed by the troops back in the Rongbuk; and during the night gusts gave the tent sporadic thrashings unconducive to peace of mind. There*

The north ridge team climb from their arete on to the north ridge. Their run of luck saw them safely past the avalanche slope and up towards the north ridge but there, alas, it ended in the mayhem of our first full-bodied winter storm. (Shaun Norman)

was no significant let-up after dawn.

The decision was made to stay where we were until conditions either improved, allowing us to continue on upwards, or deteriorated further, forcing us downwards. Outside it was relatively clear with clouds playing spaceship games on the western horizon and closer, and it was bitterly, bitterly cold. Hugh dropped in from the higher tent for an extended state-of-play and fat-chewing session. And maybe Mike did too, I don't remember. We stayed in our sleeping bags, cooked precarious meals and waited through another rather unsettling night.

We were running out of climbing time. If we didn't go upwards in the far from appetising conditions now, it would pretty well all be over unless we were prepared to stay 'in situ' and jack up our own travel arrangements back out to Lhasa. Beyond the humming fabric it was patently clear that the 'yet another' storm was more than on its way and that it really was time to admit defeat and push off. New snow was also falling, or being blown from somewhere through the now

---

Warwick Anderson, Bruce Farmer, Mike Rheinberger and Hugh Van Noorden retreat down the trough on the East Rongbuk glacier after their north ridge attempt. 'It was as if we were part of Moses's mob walking between the parted waves of the Red Sea, frozen in time and hoisted up thousands of feet in altitude.' (Shaun Norman)

---

deepening whiteout. So we discussed it, all five of us together in the big tent. Aspirations and emotions were weighed against objective cognisance of the facts — a simple situation, but very hard for each one to wrestle with internally and to control, especially for Hugh and Bruce. It was I who argued most strongly in favour of going down and Shaun for maybe holding out for a little longer.

At lunchtime that day we packed up. The wind was fierce, visibility was limited, and there was some new snow.

Again it was Hugh and Mike who forged the route. Initially it was a hundred feet of plugging directly up from the tent sites to where a five- to ten-minute traverse could be made to a Japanese flag on the ridge crest. With the newish snow and the fact that the traverse was across an open slope there was fear of avalanching, but there were no better options. Teeth were gritted and it was done one at a time. Only one person could traverse a given section at a time as little slithers of surface snow took off from some of the foot placements. Shaun had been having trouble with the larger tent which he had strapped to the outside of his pack and even after fixing this while standing precariously at the start of the traverse he was still having difficulties. The wind was hounding us all and in the streaming whiteout visibility was down to about thirty paces. Altogether a nerve-wracking exercise.

It was good to be off that traverse. One part of it was tricky and the run-out would have been a terminal one. We regrouped on the north ridge. Now on the route of the pre-War British expeditions, we headed downwards following the Japanese marker poles which loomed out of the obscurity, each exactly where needed. The snow was deep. It continued to be cold and the wind, concentrated by the hollow of the North Col, violent.

Within about an hour we stumbled down to the Col's flat section and along it to the snow cave the Japanese were using. There were several in residence. We were not invited in, but were given a brew of hot soup to keep us going until we reached their advance base camp in the East Rongbuk valley where we would be given shelter for the night.

Descending the Japanese ropes brought us down out of the wind. Immediately the situation seemed less intense or desperate. It was tiring work but almost a form of recreation after the nerve games getting out of our encampment above. Some of the lower sections of the line could be bumslid and that was recreational. But again, there was some risk of avalanche. The member of the Japanese expedition who had been killed a few weeks earlier had met his end while descending this route. But having a rope to clip on to provided a very comforting psychological crutch and blindfold for the duration.

We saw many ropes spronging through and out of snow walls in bizarre places and at weird angles. This route has been used a lot over the years and every expedition has laid and left its own network, which has gradually worked deeper and deeper into the bowels of the slope as new seasons of snow have fallen on top and the whole ice body has moved according to the dictates of gravity.

That night three or four Japanese entertained us royally at the moraine camp. We were served a three-course meal of reconstituted delicacies direct from Tokyo. Japanese food is excellent. Afterwards there was tentage for sleeping. In the morning we were given breakfast, again a pleasant Japanese meal — part of it was seaweed in a soup. It had a very subtle flavour. These Japanese ate well. The walk out to base camp took all day. It was a long way, perhaps more than 12 miles. Initially we walked along a lateral moraine. This was fairly broad at first and then became a narrow humped-up medial moraine when pushed out from the valley wall by an ice-flow coming in from the side. For a while we strode along this causeway of rock with ice all about. Then something strange occurred. Still striding along our raised road, it suddenly became a sunken road or subway with the ice rearing overhead on both sides like the walls of a cutting. It was as if we were part of Moses's mob walking between the parted waves of the Red Sea, frozen in time and hoisted up thousands of feet by orogenic uplift. I guess all the climbers who come to the East Rongbuk valley must experience similar thoughts about this accessway: a unique place to say the least. The telephone line of the 1933 expedition still lay intact along the ice, fifty-two years later.

It took several hours to reach the Japanese camp two where we sat in the snow and had lunch. Just as we arrived the camp's resident, the leader's wife, took off in running-shoes for the camp we'd just left, disappearing up our line of footsteps into poor weather. Considering the depth of soft snow along the route I wondered if she was courting frost-bite.

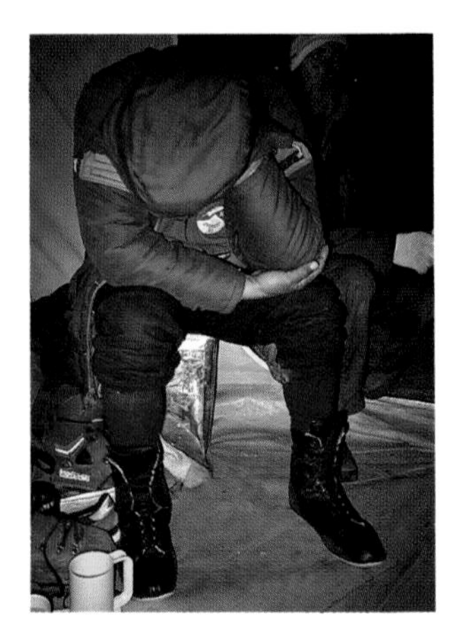

Last night at base camp. The time to be 'wound out' is now past and the time to be 'wound down' has arrived, but the tension and commitment of months take their toll.

Below the Japanese camp two a large glacier joined the East Rongbuk from the back of Changtse and the sunken moraine corridor flowed out into a much broader raised highroad. This we were able to follow almost to the end of the glacier. In general it was fast travelling. The section between the end of this moraine and the Japanese camp one, however, was not. It was hard going over very broken ground. The route was very difficult to pick out at times.
At camp one there were a few Tibetan herders with a group of yaks and also some tourists on an American Sierra Club adventure holiday. After a day of carrying packs and moraine-bashing were we glad to see them. Coffee, coffee and more coffee. From there it was less than a two-hour walk out to base camp.

On 11 October we carried the last load down to base camp. As we crossed the East Rongbuk we met Bruce and Shaun returning from their adventure over the north ridge. They looked shattered by the experience but were raving about the hospitality of the Japanese, the horrors of the eastern side of the North Col and the wonders of the East Rongbuk. It had obviously been a worthwhile trip for them.

It had been dark for an hour by the time we walked out of the moraine and on to the shingle flats near base camp. Dick and Austin met us with a hurricane lamp and a bottle of whisky. 'We're celebrating tonight,' said Austin happily. 'Julie had a son on October the 5th.'

The morning we left base camp was the fifth day of continuous snow. Winter had set in and nobody cared to linger. (Shaun Norman)

Postscript

After four years' preparation, incalculable hours of training and two months of effort on the mountain it is very hard to walk away. It's perhaps even harder to admit you were beaten, even if the fight wasn't a fair one. Maybe on Chomolungma that's all you can be certain of — that the fight won't be a fair one. But therein lies the very essence of extreme mountaineering: it is an extreme learning situation, and winning is only part of it, the occasional embellishment that puts the icing on a great effort. There is much more to learn from the mechanisms involved in working within a team, the anguish of constantly changing circumstances and the satisfaction at the end of knowing that you've exercised sound judgement.

The greatest victory of this expedition was that we mounted serious attempts on three separate routes on Chomolungma, perhaps the first expedition to ever do that, and despite one of the worst seasons for weather we survived.

Our organisation was good, we were incredibly well led by Austin and Bruce, and despite the awful conditions we kept in the main on good terms with each other — no easy task in a large team with such diverse personalities.

From my point of view I am happy to have seen so much new country and to have made so many new friends.

There is no doubt that at times we were lucky, but the real reason for our survival was not luck but good judgement. It was not luck that put our camps in places where we were given just a big fright by avalanches rather than wiped out.

So what of the future? It would be easy to become obsessed with climbing Chomolungma, indeed she has touched me with her spell and I will feel that I've got unfinished business until I am able to stand on her highest peak, but there are many other challenges too. Tibet is a place where I hope to have many more adventures, on the great rivers as well as on the mountains. While pursuing various permissions to return, I am busy in New Zealand establishing a new youth development initiative. Maybe some day I'll take a group of home-grown hoods to meet the masters of the game, the Rongbuk yak-herders, who could no doubt teach them a thing or two.

Meanwhile Bruce Farmer, Dick Price, Warwick Anderson and Mike Perry are returning to attempt the north face of Chomolungma in 1989. And the Australians Mike Rheinberger and Peter Allen will return with an Australian bicentennial expedition in 1988.

Perhaps the Goddess will be kinder.

1. LIST OF SUCCESSFUL FOREIGN EXPEDITIONS TO THE CHINESE SIDE OF CHOMOLUNGMA

TIME	TEAM	ROUTE	DATE	SUMMITERS
1980 Pre-Monsoon	Japanese Alpine Club	North Ridge	3 May	Kato Yasuo
		North Face (Japanese Direct)	10 May	Ozaki Takashi Omohiro Tsuneo
1980 Late Monsoon	Reinhold Messner solo expedition	North Ridge/ North Face	20 August	Reinhold Messner
1983 Post-Monsoon	American Everest Expedition	Kang Chung Face (East Face)	8 October	Kim Momb Carlos Buhier Lou Reichardt
			9 October	George Lowe Daniel Reid Jay Cassell
1984 Post-Monsoon	Australian Everest Expedition	North Face (Great Gully)	3 October	Tim Macartney-Snape Greg Mortimer
1984 Post-Monsoon	American Everest Expedition	North Col/ North Face	20 October	Philip Ershler
1985 Late-Monsoon	Catalan Everest Expedition	North Ridge	28 August	Carlos Valles Ocana Antonio Sors Ferrer Oscar Cadiach Puig Ang Karma (Nepali) Saambu Tameng (Nepali) Narayan Shrestha (Nepali)

2. ROUTES, RESOURCES AND ROULETTE: THE DETERMINANTS OF SUCCESS ON MT EVEREST

by Ross Cullen

During the period 1921-1985 over 100 Mt Everest expeditions took place. A handful of these had motives such as reconnaissance or ski descents of the slopes, the remainder attempted to scale the world's highest peak. Forty-one expeditions were successful in placing climbers on the summit. A total of 201 ascents were made during this period.

Although ascents of Everest no longer command the public interest, in the way they did during the 1950s and 1960s, success is far from assured for climbers venturing on to the mountain. The number of expeditions provides an adequate data base for analysis to determine if there are factors which are critical to success on Everest. The objective of this paper is to examine the data available from these expeditions to determine if there are key determinants of success, or whether random factors such as weather determine whether expeditions succeed or fail.*

Expedition objectives

Ascent of Mt Everest can be by many different routes. In a manner characteristic of mountaineering, the route of the first ascent has been joined by at least six other major routes, with several variations on these major lines. Expeditions usually choose one route, and a few groups have attempted and succeeded in climbing two routes on the mountain. There is wide acceptance among climbers that some routes are more difficult than others. The original ascent route, via the South Col, is now disparagingly called the Yak Route and is one of the easiest on the mountain. Others such as the south-west face and north-east ridge are generally accepted as posing great difficulties for climbing parties. Because of the varying nature of these different routes they are unlikely to be strictly comparable as mountaineering objectives. Hence the resource requirements for an ascent by the South Col route may be rather different from the resource requirements for the south-west face. To deal with this problem, analysis will proceed on two fronts: all expeditions grouped together, and all expeditions grouped by route(s) chosen.

Ethics and resource requirements

Expeditions to Mt Everest can be viewed as operations involving significant quantities of resources. Many writers have commented on the similarity between mountaineering expeditions and military operations. Others have suggested expedition climbing mimics business behaviour with 'radio calls replacing office memos, supply build-ups mocking corporate strategies, and problems along the way being sorted out through bureaucratic procedures.' (Fairley, 1984).

Expeditions have varied greatly in the resources they have employed for their

* Data on Everest expeditions were obtained from many sources including *Alpine Journal*, *American Alpine Journal*, *Climbing*, *Himalayan Journal*, *New Zealand Alpine Journal*. Unsworth (1981), and personal observation. The author was a member of the 1985 New Zealand Everest Expedition. Thanks are due to Bill March, University of Calgary, for assistance in obtaining data on Everest expeditions.

assaults on the mountain. Inevitably these differences in resources imply differences in costs, and the magnitudes of both resources and expedition costs have been controversial topics in mountaineering circles.

A view expressed by Tilman after the 1938 expedition — 'of course, the means must be proportional to the end .. but ... anything beyond what is needed for efficiency and safety is worse than useless' — has been espoused by many (Tilman, 1948). Others such as Reinhold Messner have asserted Everest can be 'overcome' by throwing sufficient resources into the assault. 'I know I can climb Everest with *Technik*. With enough *Technik*, so can anyone ... so many porters, so much oxygen, so many porters to carry the oxygen ... like so, I know I can climb Everest. I just as well stay at home.' (Messner quoted in Unsworth, 1981).

Mountaineers such as Messner try to avoid the 'inevitability' of success by deliberately reducing the resources employed on the mountain. This policy of scaling down expeditions conforms to the notion expressed by Tejada-Flores of changing 'games' (Tejada-Flores, 1978). Expeditions to Mt Everest can and do adopt self-imposed rules regarding the scale and style of the expedition. The 'expedition' game allows the use of almost any type of resource on the mountain, whereas the 'super-alpine' game forbids the use of porters, fixed ropes or a series of camps. A recent variation on this also forbids the use of artificial oxygen or high-altitude porters.

Obviously, these restrictions increase the uncertainty of success for expeditions. Such restrictions, generally applauded by the mountaineering fraternity, are perhaps most vehemently expressed by David Cox. 'The worthwhileness of an ascent is in inverse proportion to how much it costs, i.e. how far it is necessary to use the massive expedition approach.' (Cox, 1978). Thus, mountaineering ethics encourage economising on resources used during ascents.*

But the various routes on Everest vary in their resource requirements. Approaches from the north and east allow virtually unimpeded access to the mountain by road transport, whereas the approach through Nepal necessitates a long march from the road end, or from the nearest airfield. Thus, some differences in resources employed simply reflect different modes of transport used to approach the mountain. Trucks and yaks are invariably used during approaches from Tibet. Porters, and occasionally helicopters, are employed during approaches through Nepal. Means of transport to base camps are of little consequence in determining success on the mountain, and are ignored in the analysis which follows.

Stochastic elements

Mountaineering is a hazardous activity and success is uncertain. Because of this uncertainty, one factor beyond all others is required for success.

> *The climbers must have above all things, if they are to win through, good fortune, and the greatest good fortune of all for mountaineers, some constant spirit of kindness in Mount Everest itself, the forgetfulness*

* A more detailed examination of the relationship between mountaineering ethics and efficiency, and the determinants of expedition size, is contained in another forthcoming paper.

for long enough of its more cruel moods. (Mallory quoted in Ahluwalia, 1978).

Luck will always be a factor influencing expeditions to Mt Everest, and luck most clearly manifests itself in the weather which greets climbers. Weather in the Himalaya is strongly influenced by the monsoon and two main climbing seasons have developed: pre-monsoon and post-monsoon. Only a handful of expeditions have attempted the mountain during the monsoon period, and a similarly small number of expeditions have been tempted to climb during the winter months.

Expeditions can be grouped by the season they choose for their attempt on the mountain, and successes compared. Two criteria are employed to measure success: the proportion of expeditions which succeed in placing one or more climbers on the summit, and the average number of climbers per expedition who reach the summit.

As Table 1 indicates, a simple indicator of success — did the expedition succeed in placing someone on top — suggests there is little difference between seasons. But this indicator conceals more than it reveals, and the second criterion — number of ascents per expedition — reveals substantial differences between the seasons.

TABLE 1: SUCCESS BY SEASON

Season	Number of Expeditions	Expeditions Successful	Climbers Successful	Expedition Success Ratio (%)	Ascents per Expedition
Pre-Monsoon	50	21	121	42.0	2.42
Monsoon	5	2	7	40.0	1.40
Post-Monsoon	35	15	60	42.8	1.88
Winter	9	3	7	35.0	0.77
Total	99	41	201	41.4	2.0

The pre-monsoon season has long been regarded as the most favourable for climbing, and clearly has the highest ratio of ascents per expedition. Winter, the harshest season, encourages only the most hardy, perhaps foolhardy, to try, and thus expedition sizes are small and the number of successful ascents per expedition low.

A second mode of analysis is to examine the effect of season on success ratios for different routes. Season may have a much more dramatic effect on some routes than on others. One obvious reason for this is changes in the prevailing wind and the effect on snow conditions during the various seasons. Winds on Everest are typically from the west and reach their climax during the winter when the jet-stream airflows batter the mountain, stripping it of snow. The prevailing westerly wind results in heavier snow accumulation on the northern and eastern slopes — the leeward slopes — of Mt Everest than on the southern slopes. Snow accumulation increases avalanche risk, slows progress on the mountain, and may be an important determinant of success. Snow accumulates during the monsoon period and so the post-monsoon period is most prone to excess snow. The pre-monsoon period, following as it does the winter winds, typically has much less snow.

One obvious grouping is leeward-slope routes and windward-slope routes. Leeward-slope routes include the west ridge, the Hornbein direct, the north face, north ridge, north-east ridge and east face. All other routes are windward-slope routes. Table 2 provides a breakdown of data by season for leeward and windward slope routes. Although this does show a remarkable difference between leeward and windward slope success ratios, it does not reveal any tendency for leeward slopes to be more difficult in the post-monsoon than in the pre-monsoon period.

TABLE 2: SUCCESS BY SEASON BY LEEWARD AND WINDWARD ROUTES

Post-Monsoon and Monsoon

Route	Number of Expeditions	Expeditions Successful	Climbers Successful	Expedition Success Ratios (%)	Climbers Successful per Expedition
Leeward Routes	20	6	18	30.0	0.90
West Ridge	6	0	0	0.0	0.00
North Face	4	2	3	50.0	0.75
North Ridge	8	3	9	37.5	1.12
East Face	2	1	6	50.0	3.00
All Windward Routes	20	11	55	55.0	2.75

Pre-Monsoon

Route	Number of Expeditions	Expeditions Successful	Climbers Successful	Expedition Success Ratios (%)	Climbers Successful per Expedition
Leeward Routes	29	6	27	20.7	0.93
West Ridge	8	3	12	37.5	1.50
North Face	3	1	3	33.0	1.00
North Ridge	16	2	12	12.5	0.75
North-east Ridge	2	0	0	0.0	0.00
All Windward Routes	21	15	94	71.4	4.47

Route

We now focus more closely on success ratios on different routes. Table 3 provides a breakdown of ascents by route chosen. Where expeditions had multiple objectives, as the 1963 American Expedition did, they are recorded as separate expeditions to each objective. This breakdown provides insights into expedition objectives and explanations for expedition successes.

Over 37 percent of all expeditions to Everest have attempted to climb by the standard South Col route, 65 percent of all successful expeditions to the mountain have followed that route, and 70 percent of all ascents have been by that route. Clearly this is a relatively easy route where the requirements for success are well known, and large expeditions now queue up to make their attempts. These comments are supported by other statistics. Seventy percent of all expeditions attempting the South Col/South Pillar route have succeeded in placing climbers on the summit. Ascents per expedition which attempt this route average 3.53, almost double the figure for any other route apart from the east face.

The second most popular route, the north ridge, has attracted 24.5 percent of all expeditions to the mountain but only 16 percent of expedition successes and only 10.9 percent of successful ascents have been by this route. It was the original and only route attempted before 1952, and saw eleven failures before Everest was climbed by the South Col route in 1953. It remained unclimbed until the Chinese success of 1960.

Removing the pre-1953 attempts from the analysis substantially changes the success indicators for the north ridge. Forty-seven percent of all expeditions on the north ridge have succeeded since 1953, with an average of 1.47 ascents per expedition. These figures suggest the north ridge is not particularly difficult, using modern techniques and knowledge, a point clearly demonstrated by the solo and oxygenless ascent made by this route by Messner in 1980.

The third ridge route on Everest, the west ridge, has attracted eighteen expeditions but only three have succeeded. Only the north-east ridge appears to equal the west ridge in difficulty. They share some characteristics: both are very long routes, both have their crux above 24,000 feet and both are on the leeward side of the mountain and thus prone to heavy snow accumulations. These routes seem to be unlikely candidates for oxygenless ascents and safe returns, for they demand major physical efforts at high altitude and do not allow rapid descents to lower altitudes except by other routes. The north-east ridge remains the last unclimbed ridge on Everest.

There are three major faces on Everest: the south-west, north and east. The south-west face has a reputation for extreme difficulty which is only partly supported by the success indicators in Table 3. Concealed in these summary statistics are the massive quantities of resources required to succeed on this route. Some of the largest, and most costly, Everest expeditions have been directed at the south-west face. The two successful south-west face expeditions, the British in 1975 and the Russian in 1982, each cost £130,000 and involved over 1,000 people. The reasons for these massive quantities of resources are not very clear, for the route appears to present similar difficulties to the west and north-east ridges, which have been attempted by expeditions with considerably fewer resources.

The north face and east face routes have only recently been attempted as Tibet was officially closed to expeditions from 1949 to 1980. Both these routes are subject to huge snow build-ups as they are on the leeward slopes. The objective danger owing to avalanches is likely to be high, as several expeditions have discovered. But face routes tend to be very direct routes to the summit, and this combined with ease of access to the beginning of these routes reduces the quantity of resources required. For these two routes luck may be the key determinant of success, for snow conditions must be good to allow rapid safe movement up the

TABLE 3: SUCCESS BY ROUTE

Route	Number of Expeditions†	Expeditions Successful††	Climbers Successful†††	Expedition Success Ratio (%)	Ascents per Expedition
South Col/ South Pillar	40	28	141	70.0	3.53
South-west Face	9	2	16	22.2	1.77
West Ridge	18	3	12	16.6	0.66
North Face	9	2	4	22.2	0.44
North Ridge	26	7	22	26.9	0.85
—			Post 1953	46.6	1.47
North-east Ridge	2	0	0	0.0	0.00
East Face	2	1	6	50.0	3.00
	106	43	201	40.6	1.89

† The total of expeditions exceeds the actual number of 99, because some expeditions had several objectives and are listed for each separate route. It is also assumed that the 1952 Russian and 1966 Chinese expeditions took place.

†† Success is attributed by route ascended.

††† It is assumed M. Burke reached the summit in 1975.

long slopes. Pre-monsoon expeditions to these face routes will reduce avalanche danger, but access can be difficult because of crevasses en route.

This analysis of success by route chosen provides very clear evidence of the degree of difficulty attached to some routes compared to the 'standard' South Col route. Expedition success can be strongly influenced by route chosen. As Table 2 shows, over 75 percent of all expeditions on leeward slope routes failed compared to 37 percent on windward slope routes. This simple division may be the most powerful single explanation for success and failure on Everest.

Resources

Expeditions combine inputs of time, effort and equipment to produce outputs of attempts on high peaks, and sometimes successful ascents. It seems reasonable to speculate that there may be a relationship between the magnitudes of inputs and outputs. Climbers typically seem to focus only on the number of climbers in an expedition, as a measure of its size. This is likely to provide a very misleading measure of expedition capabilities, if other inputs are substitutes for climbers or significantly aid in making ascents. Obviously substitutes for climbers' efforts exist and are usually employed on expeditions. Sherpas, winches and helicopters have all been used to assist with load carrying on Mt Everest and must be included in a comprehensive measure of total resources employed by expeditions. Other inputs, clothing, tents, food, ropes, crampons, ice axes and so forth, are also essential for a successful ascent of the world's highest peak. As the quotation from Messner above suggests, many climbers believe that by increasing the quantity of resources employed by an expedition, the probability of success can also be increased.

If data existed on total resources employed by expeditions to Everest, this hypothesis could be tested. The most obvious, comprehensive measure of resources employed is the total cost of expeditions. Unfortunately, obtaining comparable data on total costs for expeditions is a difficult task. Expedition budgets as reported in mountaineering literature are poor indicators of total resources employed because of the subsidisation of many input costs, and zero price for some inputs, notably climbers' time. Further impediments to the use of data on total costs are the unavailability of reliable data, and the need for many deflators and exchange rates to allow comparison of data from different years and different countries. Although these are not insurmountable problems, they are sufficient to allow only cursory comment about total costs in this paper.

Table 4 lists data on costs for seventeen expeditions. Perhaps the most striking feature of this data is the extreme variation in average cost per expedition member, with the most costly expedition, the 1980 Japanese expedition, costing twenty times Earl Denman's 1947 expedition. Expeditions of similar size and from similar eras also differ widely in average cost, e.g. the 1956 Swiss and 1963 American expeditions, and the 1985 Spanish and 1985 New Zealand expeditions. Variation in Sherpa numbers is not sufficient to explain these cost differences.

Is there any evidence showing a positive relationship between costs and expedition success? Comparison of expeditions is fraught with difficulty, for resource requirements may differ significantly between routes. The south-west face, for example, has attracted only expeditions with very large budgets compared to almost all other routes. The evidence available on expedition costs hints that large-budget expeditions have a greater probability of success, but the data base is too small to draw any firm conclusions.

TABLE 4: COSTS OF SOME SELECTED EVEREST EXPEDITIONS

Year	Nationality	Route	Number of Climbers	Total Cost 1985 $(US)	Average Cost per Climber 1985 $(US)
1922	British	North Ridge	8	384,528	48,066
1933	British	North Ridge	14	414,470	29,605
1938	British	North Ridge	7	74,704	10,672
1947	Canadian	North Ridge	1	4,330	4,330
1956	Swiss	South Col	11	310,518	28,229
1963	USA	West Ridge/ South Col	20	1,311,800	65,590
1972	British	South-west Face	11	360,250	32,750
1975	British	South-west Face	18	539,172	29,954
1976	British/Nepal	South Col	34	635,528	18,692
1976	USA	South Col	12	353,088	29,424
1977	New Zealand	South Col	8	64,304	8,038
1978	Austrian	South Col	11	193,116	17,556
1980	Japanese	North Face/ North Ridge	26	2,274,038	87,463
1982	Canadian	South Pillar	16	423,488	26,468
1985	Spanish	North Ridge	18	824,994	45,833
1985	French	North Face	3	30,249	10,083
1985	New Zealand	West Ridge	14	82,502	5,893

Table 5 presents partial correlation coefficients between four measures of expedition resources and number of ascents. These results suggest that greater quantities of resources, particularly numbers of Sherpas, do lead to a greater probability of success on Mt Everest. But it cannot be claimed that success can be guaranteed by increasing the size of the expedition. A multiple regression analysis of the number of climbers, number of Sherpas, route and season can explain at most 25 percent of the variation in the numbers of ascents different expeditions achieve. The unavoidable conclusion is that success on Everest is still largely dependent on factors such as weather, snow conditions and luck.

What does seem clear is that it is possible to mount small-scale low-cost expeditions to Everest using modern climbing styles. This possibility was demonstrated first by the 1938 British expedition, and has been vindicated by the successful ascents of Everest by one-, five-, and six-person expeditions in 1980, 1984 and 1983 respectively.

So Messner's belief that large expeditions can guarantee success on Everest appears to be unsupported by the data. He appears to have reconsidered his position and has since stated, 'I feel the chances of success are largely the same, whether an expedition is big or small.' (Messner, 1978)

TABLE 5: PARTIAL CORRELATION COEFFICIENTS

	Number of Climbers†	Number of Sherpas†	Average Cost††	Total Cost††
Number of Ascents	.1020	.2454*	.6042*	-0.3832

† 89 observations
†† 18 observations
* significant at r = .05

Oxygen or your life?

Linked to the question of resources and success on Everest is the question of the use of artificial oxygen. There is no doubt concerning the efficacy of oxygen at altitude. The advantage it granted to the climber was clearly demonstrated by Finch during the 1922 attempt on the mountain. Debate concerning its use has focused on two topics: is it ethical, and are the logistical problems it poses so great as to outweigh the advantages it provides?

The ethical question has long been debated, among both climbers and non-climbers. A non-climber declared of the 1924 expedition, 'If some of the party do not go to 25,000 feet without oxygen they will be rotters' (Hinks quoted in Unsworth, 1981, p. 531). Climbers who value their lives may have slightly different views on this subject. Many of the pre-1953 attempts on Everest were made without the use of oxygen, but the success of the 1953 expedition did establish a pattern of oxygen-assisted expeditions which lasted until 1978. Since the first oxygenless ascent, ethical debate has resumed. Habeler and Messner demonstrated Everest could be climbed without oxygen, and in climbing 'could' comes to mean 'should'. Several expeditions, and groups within expeditions, have succeeded in climbing

Everest without oxygen since 1978, thus reinforcing the idea that this is the 'ethical' approach to Everest.

Supporting the ethical argument is the argument from the point of view of logistics or efficiency. Artificial oxygen is heavy, cumbersome stuff. Carrying cylinders to high altitudes in readiness for a dash to the summit adds to the load-carrying problems facing expeditions. If expeditions have only a limited capacity to carry loads of tents, food, gas, ropes and other gear to altitude, the use of oxygen may mean the expedition succeeds in carrying the oxygen to altitude, but at the cost of so wearying expedition members that they are unable to continue on to the summit. Thus a decision to avoid use of oxygen allows expeditions to conserve their energies for climbing, reduces the number of loads to be carried and hence reduces the number of porters and Sherpas required, and thus the total cost of the expedition. Oxygenless ascents are supported on both ethical and efficiency grounds.

But there are limits to the physiological ability of man and the summit of Mt Everest is very close to the limit of altitude at which man can survive without artificial oxygen. (West, 1984). The ascents of Everest without artificial oxygen should be read in conjunction with the evidence of fatalities on oxygenless ascents.

Everest has claimed a large number of lives, on average one for every expedition which has attempted the mountain. Table 6 shows deaths by route chosen, and reveals that 79 percent of all deaths have occurred on expeditions with either the south-east ridge or north ridge as their objective. There is some doubt about the accuracy of the data, for the deaths on the north ridge of six Russian climbers in 1952 and twenty-four Chinese climbers in 1966 have not been officially confirmed. But a considerable price has obviously been paid for the successes achieved on Everest.

But of greater relevance are the figures on fatalities amongst climbers not using oxygen, compared to those for climbers using oxygen. The critical altitude for oxygen deprivation is alleged to be above 23,000 feet, sometimes called the 'death zone'. The final day of ascents is the period when hypoxia assumes major importance. We focus therefore on fatalities amongst climbers on their 'summit day'. Of the fatalities listed in Table 6 five are climbers who reached the summit

TABLE 6: DEATHS BY ROUTE

Route	Number of Expeditions	Number of Deaths*	Deaths per Expedition
South Col/South Pillar	41	34	0.83
South-west Face	9	3	0.33
West Ridge	18	14	0.78
North Face	9	3	0.33
North Ridge	25	47	1.88
North-east Ridge	2	2	1.00
East Face	2	0	0.00
	106	103	0.97

* Assumes 6 Russian climbers died in 1952 and 24 Chinese climbers in 1966.

with oxygen but perished on the descent, and a further three using oxygen are believed to have died while making summit attempts. Four climbers have died after making oxygenless ascents, and at least seven others have died during oxygenless summit attempts. Altogether 181 ascents of Mt Everest have been completed with oxygen assistance and twenty ascents have been completed without artificial oxygen. The ratio of deaths to ascents is therefore 5/181 (2.7 percent) using oxygen, as opposed to 4/20 (20 percent) not using oxygen. Adding those who died during summit attempts results in ratios of 8/184 (4.3 percent) and 11/37 (29.7 percent) respectively. Although these latter figures may not include all summit attempts, the evidence is startlingly clear. Climbing without oxygen greatly increases the probability of death. The new harder ethics of the super-alpine game have harsh effects on Mt Everest. Climbers contemplating oxygenless ascents of Everest would be well advised to consider the wisdom of their decision. Intrinsic difficulty and length of both ascent and descent routes may be critical in determining where oxygenless ascents are least hazardous (West, 1984).

Nationality

Expeditions to Everest are not private affairs. National prestige is often at stake and many countries have viewed ascents of Everest as symbols of nationhood or national character. If expeditions are categorised by the nationality of their organisers, or prime movers, expeditions from twenty-seven countries have attempted Everest together with two 'international' expeditions. Clearly Everest is no longer, if it ever was, a 'British' mountain.

Three countries dominate the supply of expeditions — Great Britain, Japan and the USA. As Table 7 shows, almost half of all expeditions have originated in those three countries. A further three countries have mounted five or more expeditions — France, Spain and India. The remaining thirty-three expeditions are spread amongst twenty-one countries and the two international expeditions. Seven countries have attempted to climb Everest only once.

Comparison of success ratios between countries is fraught with problems because of differences in difficulty of objective attempted. This may at least partly explain the startling differences in success ratios between British and French expeditions, and Japanese and American expeditions. Similarly the lack of success by New Zealand expeditions may reflect a deficiency of resources for the objectives chosen, rather than any deficiencies among the climbers themselves.

Nationals of at least twenty-three countries have now ascended Mt Everest, surely dispelling any notion that only nationals of a few countries are capable of high-altitude mountaineering. Noticeably, however, thirty-eight of the 201 ascents have been by Nepali climbers acting in their capacity of paid assistants to expeditions from other countries. More Nepalis have ascended Mt Everest than nationals of any other country, clearly reflecting their greater opportunities for ascent because of their participation on many expeditions to Everest.

TABLE 7: SUCCESS BY NATIONALITY OF EXPEDITION

Country	Number of Expeditions*	Expeditions Successful	Climbers Successful	Expedition Success Ratio (%)	Climbers Successful per Expedition
Argentina	1	0	0	0.0	0.00
Australia	2	1	2	50.0	1.00
Austria	1	1	9	100.0	9.00
Britain	18	3	9	16.6	0.50
Bulgaria	1	1	5	100.0	5.00
Canada	2	1	6	50.0	3.00
Chile	1	0	0	0.0	0.00
China	3	2	12	66.6	4.00
Czechoslovakia	1	1	3	100.0	3.00
Denmark	1	0	0	0.0	0.00
France	8	1	4	12.5	0.50
Germany	2	2	25	100.0	12.50
India	5	2	14	40.0	2.80
Iran	1	0	0	0.0	0.00
Italy	3	2	9	66.6	3.00
Japan	13	9	23	69.2	1.77
International	2	0	0	0.0	0.00
Nepal	2	0	0	0.0	0.00
Netherlands	2	1	1	50.0	0.50
New Zealand	4	0	0	0.0	0.00
Norway	1	1	17	100.0	17.00
Poland	2	2	4	100.0	2.00
Russia	2	1	11	50.0	5.50
South Korea	2	1	2	50.0	1.00
Spain	5	2	8	40.0	1.60
Switzerland	4	1	4	25.0	1.00
USA	14	6	28	42.9	2.00
Yugoslavia	1	1	5	100.0	5.00

* Joint expeditions are credited to both countries.

Personal characteristics

Persons living at high altitudes do have some physiological differences from lowlanders, and may be better suited for high altitude climbing. Because they live all year-round above 12,000 feet, Sherpas and Tamangs begin expeditions already acclimatised. Climbers arriving from lower altitudes typically need six weeks to adjust to the lower air pressure. The frequency of ascents by Sherpas and Tamangs, and their successes without artificial oxygen, suggest they may be better suited to the challenges posed by Everest. But the notion that Everest climbers are super-athletes has little medical support. Psychological traits may be more important than physiological capability, for several decades of medical research have failed to find a physiological predictor for high-altitude performance.

Age has not proven to be a barrier to ascent of Everest, for climbers from eighteen to fifty-five years have succeeded. Sex differences have likewise been dismissed as a possible barrier, for at least five women have now climbed Everest.

Expeditions do push their strongest, most able climbers to the front, to maximise the chances of expedition success. The presence of strong, well-acclimatised climbers on an expedition may be necessary for success, but it is not sufficient to guarantee expeditions are successful. Stochastic factors such as weather and snow conditions can negate the chances of even the strongest and most able climbers.

Conclusion

Analysis of Everest expedition data provides only modest amounts of evidence that we can use to explain why some expeditions succeed and others fail. Choice of route and quantity of resources available appear to have some explanatory power, but much of the variation in numbers of ascents remains unexplained. Presently unquantified factors such as monsoon intensity, snow conditions and psychological traits of climbers may be required to provide better explanations of success and failure. Chance may still be the prime determinant of success on Everest.

REFERENCES

Ahluwalia, H.P.S. (1970) *Faces of Everest,* Vikas Publishing House, New Delhi.

Alpine Journal, several volumes.

American Alpine Journal, several volumes.

Baume, L. (1978) *Sivalaya,* Gaston-West Col, Goring.

Burgess, A. (1985) 'Nepal — Mecca for the Himalayan Climber' in *Climbing,* (91) 51-57.

Climbing, several volumes.

Cox, D. (1978) 'Some comments on an Everest book' in *The Games Climbers Play* (edited by K. Wilson), Diadem Books, London, 375-377.

Cullen, R. (forthcoming) 'Efficiency, Ethics and Expedition Size'.

Fairley, B. (1984) 'Mountaineering and the ethics of technique' in *Canadian Alpine Journal,* (14) 49-52.

Himalayan Journal, several volumes.

Messner, Rheinhold (1978) 'A Second Talk with Messner' in *The Games Climbers Play* (edited by K. Wilson), Diadem Books, London, 380-388.

Mountain, several volumes.

Tejada-Flores, L. (1978) 'Games Climbers Play' in *The Games Climbers Play* (edited by K. Wilson), Diadem Books, London, 19-27.

Tilman, H.W. (1948) *Mount Everest 1938,* Cambridge University Press, Cambridge.

Unsworth, W. (1981) *Everest.* Allen Lane, London.

West, J.B. (1984) 'Oxygenless Climbs and Barometric Pressure' in *American Alpine Journal,* (26) 126-133.

Wilson, K. (1978) ed. *The Games Climbers Play,* Diadem Books, London.

3. BUDGET PLANNING FOR EXPEDITIONS TO THE CHINESE SIDE OF CHOMOLUNGMA
by Austin Brookes

One of the advantages of organising an expedition to China is that it is possible to budget very precisely. Costs may be high but they are predictable. Naturally the Chinese Mountaineering Association will not regard a budget submitted to them as a contract but the submitted budget does allow the expedition to check expenditure while it is in progress.

On that basis costs can be estimated at 9-10,000 yuan per expedition member in China, assuming that there is no need to maintain contact with the outside world. If it is considered necessary to have a jeep and driver at base camp then a further 1-2,000 yuan per expedition member must be added on. These figures can only be achieved by very careful control of expenditure. On our expedition only two people had the authority to authorise expenditure on behalf of the expedition.

Team members must apply quite a rigorous self-discipline. A climber who becomes ill because of poor acclimatisation could generate quite hefty costs. Similarly there have to be quite rigid limits to the amount of personal gear. This meant arriving in Beijing in 40°C dressed in heavy climbing clothing and in-flight baggage of 30 pounds each.

When planning food and equipment in New Zealand the weight and volume must not exceed one truckload. A second truck would have meant an extra 2,000 yuan per member. This means that there cannot be unlimited spare food, luxury items or numerous spare pieces of equipment.

Unfortunately too, accommodation costs mean that it is expensive to spend much time in the settlements. One simply cannot (at 120 yuan per person per day) spend much time in Lhasa. Time for acclimatisation is therefore short and individuals must exercise great restraint. This is difficult in such an exciting country.

It is the possibilities of illness owing to poor acclimatisation or owing to an accident on the mountain that have the greatest potential for cost escalation. It makes it vital to have a very comprehensive medical kit, and a doctor like Dick Price is almost literally worth his weight in gold.

The budget submitted to the Chinese Mountaineering Association for this expedition follows. In fact a sympathetic Chinese Mountaineering Association and a very good liaison officer helped us beat this by over 10 percent. Unfortunately the accident to Mike Andrews put us back to square one. One should, I believe, always add in a 10 percent for contingencies as well as arrange comprehensive evacuation insurance.

BUDGET PROPOSED FOR 1985 NEW ZEALAND EXPEDITION TO CHOMOLUNGMA

		Yuan
Peak fee (paid)		4,000.00
Liaison Officer and Interpreter		
Subsidy 91 x 32 x 2		5,824.00
Insurance (death)		1,000.00
Insurance (medical)		200.00
Food 75 x 22 x 2		3,300.00
Travel		
Beijing-Chengdu (train)		
185 x 2 x 2		740.00
Chengdu-Lhasa (air)		
322 x 2 x 2		1,288.00
Food on train (say)		100.00
Equipment (provided by CMA) 500 x 2		1,000.00
Accommodation		
Beijing 6 x 90 x 2		1,080.00
Chengdu 3 x 90 x 2		540.00
Lhasa 3 x 240 x 2		1,440.00
Xigatse 3 x 120 x 2		720.00
Xegar 2 x 60 x 2		240.00
		21,472.00
	5% CMA commission	1,073.60
		22,545,60
Yaks		
Inward 12 yaks		
Hire 12 x 6 x 30		2,160.00
Driver — subsidy 2 x 6 x 16		192.00
— food 2 x 6 x 17		204.00
Insurance (death)		300.00
Insurance (medical)		100.00
Equipment 200 x 2		400.00
Travelling fee 2 x 40		80.00
Outward 6 yaks		
Hire 6 x 6 x 30		1,080.00
Driver — subsidy 1 x 6 x 16		96.00
— food 1 x 6 x 17		102.00
Insurance (death)		150.00
Insurance (medical)		50.00
Equipment 1 x 200		200.00
Travelling fee 1 x 40		40.00
		5,154.00
	5% CMA commission	257.70
		5,411.70

Equipment in China

Fuel 750 l kerosene @ 1.26 per litre	945.00
Duty on food and equipment. *(Note:* All food and equipment is donated to expedition.) Value nominal. Duty (say)	500.00
Equipment transport 2,500 kg Beijing-Lhasa (includes food for Liaison Officer and interpreter to be provided by CMA) @ 5.48/kg	13,700.00
Excess baggage carried by expedition members in	
350 kg (by train Beijing-Chengdu @ 1.13/kg)	395.50
350 kg (by air Chengdu-Lhasa @ 3.32/kg)	1,162.00
Excess baggage accompanying expedition members out	
500 kg (by air Lhasa-Chengdu @ 3.32/kg)	1,660.00
500 kg (by train Chengdu-Beijing @ 1.13/kg)	565.00
Container of food and equipment to be delivered to CMA three months prior to expedition arrival. Unloading at Tientsin and cartage to Beijing	4,850.00
	23,777.50
5% CMA commission	1,188.90
	24,966.40

Vehicle Transport in Tibet

(1,800 km Lhasa-base camp and return)	
Truck 4.8 x 1800 x 1.5	12,960.00
Coach (2nd class) 6.4 x 1800 x 1.5	17,280.00
Road fees — truck and coach - 2 x 2000	4,000.00
Note: Toyota (NZ) will be able to supply jeep for expedition.	
	34,240.00
5% CMA commission	1,712.00
	35,952.00

Travel by Expedition Members

Beijing-Chengdu (train) 185 x 14 x 2	5,180.00
Chengdu-Lhasa (air) 322 x 14 x 2	9,016.00
Food on train (say)	700.00

Accommodation

Beijing 6 x 90 x 14		7,560.00
Chengdu 3 x 90 x 14		3,780.00
Lhasa 3 x 210 x 14		8,820.00
Xigatse 3 x 120 x 14		5,040.00
Xegar 1 x 60 x 14		1,680.00
		41,776.00
	5% CMA commission	2,088.80
		43,864.80
TOTAL		132,740.50

4. PHOTOGRAPHY ON CHOMOLUNGMA
by Mike Perry

The mountain environment is demanding on film and cameras but does provide one major assistance usually lacking in more congenial places — an abundance of light.

The finest grain, sharpest and best colour-saturated films always have a slow film speed, i.e. ISO rating. In your average city street it's a struggle to use these films and maintain adequate shutter speed, particularly when taking telephoto shots. One has the options of using very expensive and heavy, wide maximum-aperture lenses, or higher ISO film that gives lesser picture quality. Up above the snowline there's so much light that one can comfortably use not only ISO 64 or even ISO 25 film, but also zoom lenses whose relatively small maximum apertures make them undesirable for low-light shooting.

I considered a number of films for our expedition and found that the best all-round film was Kodachrome 64. E6 process films such as Ektachrome 64 are actually just as good but more tricky to use and sensitive to poor storage. I did shoot Ektachrome wherever possible when photographing our sponsors' products because its rich colours make for more exciting pictures.

Kodachrome's major limitations are its poor highlight contrast, which gives a nasty 'blown-out' look to over-exposed snow and clouds, and a tendency towards significant colour-shift when using very slow shutter speeds. Neither of these problems was relevant to our use of the film. Bright snow and cloud are more likely to cause under-exposure than over-exposure of film, and the light is so bright that shutter speeds are always fast.

I did use Ektachrome 400 pushed to ISO 800 on one occasion in a dark monastery prayer room. It is a matter of personal taste but I like to use existing light in preference to flash for low-light illustrative photography. In this case, using film set at ISO 800 still meant a shutter speed of 1/4 second, and Kodachrome 64 was obviously inappropriate.

One should always use a filter as protection over the camera lens. An ultra-violet (U.V.) filter is the choice for most situations when using Kodachrome. It is also handy to have a polarising filter for cutting back haze or reflection and adding drama to clouds and blue sky.

We had the usual variety of camera brands and they all seemed to be adequate but I would suggest that Nikon, Minolta and Canon are the cameras with the best chance of standing up to the mountains. From personal experience I know that Nikon cameras and lenses have a durability that is almost incredible. However, the most important consideration with a camera for the mountains is not the brand but the level of gadgetry. If you love technology then get a space-age camera with an on-board computer and flashing lights, but if you want a camera that will operate reliably and predictably for years then get a fully manual camera from a reputable manufacturer.

Simple cameras are the most reliable and these cameras have only manual light metering. Judging exposure on snow is really easy once you have the knack, and is an exercise more likely to fool some high-tech multi-mode automatic metering system than you.

Lenses are a matter of personal taste but for mountaineers zoom lenses have considerable virtue. When you're staggering under a heavy pack and a hot sun, feel like you're getting frost-bite, or are on your hands and knees at 28,000 feet, chances are you're surrounded by amazing scenes but the lens you need is out of reach in your pack. Compact zooms overcome the problem of changing lenses in blizzards, or even changing at all, do not mean much extra weight and still provide excellent optical quality.

On Chomolungma, as in the New Zealand mountains, I used two zooms, 35-70 mm and 80-200 mm. The 35-70 mm lens was very small and light, making it suitable for situations where weight was critical; its focal length range was ideal for both people and landscape pictures. The 80-200 mm lens was rather heavier and tended to be left behind when major suffering owing to pack weight was anticipated.

The key to a satisfactory choice of zoom is to buy a brand name lens, i.e. if you own a Minolta camera buy a Minolta lens. Moreover, don't fall into the trap of buying some monstrous 28 mm-200 mm zoom, it will be so heavy and bulky that you'll hate it. Get the lightest zoom in the range.

A couple of technical points relating to our experiences on Chomolungma. Camera batteries are very prone to malfunction in the cold, so keep your camera warm and carry a spare battery in a shirt pocket. Secondly, watch for condensation in the lens if you take a camera from a warm place, such as inside a down suit, to cold air. Film is also affected by cold (and heat), so wind it on carefully as really cold film will become brittle and break.

Lastly a number of us took Nikon fixed-lens cameras featuring auto-focus, auto-exposure, auto-wind and auto-rewind. The cameras are fragile and require large batteries but in really disgusting conditions can be operated with one heavily gloved hand whereas a single lens reflex camera cannot. It is the one appropriate use for an automatic camera in the mountains!

5. GLOSSARY

Abseiling
Also called 'rapelling'. Descending a rope secured from above. One's speed of descent is controlled by the friction of the rope either around the body or threaded through a descending device attached to the body harness.

Arete
A sharp ridge that may be found on a face or flank of a major ridge, but usually not in itself a major feature of the mountain.

Avalanche
A windslab avalanche occurs where a wind-packed layer of snow fails to bond to the snow beneath. When this slab is stressed, usually either by someone climbing on it, by a temperature change or by the weight of additional snow falling on top of it, a fracture occurs at the point of maximum stress and the slab tumbles down hill.

A powder avalanche is simply the release of an accumulation of unconsolidated powder snow. The key factors determining the likelihood of powder avalanches are the angle of the slope, the depth of the snow and the condition of the snow crystals. Powder avalanches are doubly hazardous as they generate a massive air shock-wave that can be destructive far beyond the extent of the actual snow debris.

Belaying
Securing the rope through a tie-on point (to the mountain) while another climber, tied to the rope, moves.

Bergschrund
A crevasse that forms where snow or ice meet rock, or where the angle of a snow or ice slope changes. It may also form where a glacier meets a mountain face.

Break
Also called 'headwall'. Fracture line marking release point of an avalanche.

Carabiner
Very strong aluminium shackle with a sprung gate. It is used for clipping a climbing rope to a waist-harness or to a belay.

Col
A low point on a high mountain ridge which is usually accessible from one but not necessarily both sides.

Cornice
A snow overhang formed as wind blows snow along a ridge and sweeps it over on the leeward side so that it cantilevers out over the slope below.

Couloir
A gully.

Crampon
A frame with steel spikes up to 1 1/4" long which is strapped or clipped to the boot. It is used to give secure purchase on ice and hard snow.

Crevasse
A split in the surface of a glacier or ice field. Crevasses are stress fractures in the ice, occurring where the glacier moves over uneven ground. They may be hundreds of feet deep. After a snowfall, crevasses are usually hidden and easy to fall into, hence the practice of climbers roping together on a glacier.

Cwm
A narrow, glaciated valley.

Glacier Wand
Marker pole, usually bamboo or PVC tube about 6 feet long. It is used to mark the way through an area where visibility or snowfall may make route-finding difficult.

Jumar
A mechanical device which, by use of a camming system, can be pushed up a suspended rope but not pulled down. They are used in pairs for ascending fixed ropes.

'Penitentes'
Ice pinnacles carved out by the action of sun and wind. They are so-called because they look like bowed-down people kneeling at prayer.

Recce
Reconnaissance.

Run Out
A section of climbing, the distance of which is determined by the length of the climbing rope. It is also the path of a climber's fall caused by slipping or avalanche.

Runner
Also called 'running belay'. A device which is solidly attached to the mountain and to which the climbing rope is connected by a carabiner. These devices range from rock and ice pitons (pegs), which are driven in to the rock, to aluminium wedges which are jammed in rock cracks.

Scroggin
Snack food made of a mixture of nuts, chocolate, dried fruits, sweets and so on.

Serac
A free-standing column or wall of ice found in steep, tumbling sections of glaciers. Seracs are prone to collapse without warning and can be very dangerous.

Spindrift
Wind-blown snow.

Step Plugging
Making a trail through deep snow.

Telemark Turn
A turning technique used with three-pin skis.

Three-Pin Skis
Also known as Nordic or 'skinny' skis. Light, thin skis developed in Scandinavia for cross-country travel. Only the toe of the boot is attached to the ski, usually by three metal pins and a clamp device.

Whiteout
Zero visibility caused by thick mist or snowfall.

6. ACKNOWLEDGEMENTS

It is an impossible task to acknowledge all the help given to the expedition. Our failure to reach the summit of Chomolungma makes it even more difficult to accept this impossibility, for there remains a sense (however irrational) of letting down those who gave so freely of their time and money to help us.

I can only mention specifically a few individuals and organisations whose support was crucial. I cannot set any order of precedence. How can anyone make a comparative estimate of the value of a cash contribution from a major New Zealand company with, for instance, the hours spent making snowstakes by Kingswell High School students.

The two presidents and the secretary of the New Zealand Alpine Club were unstinting in their support. Their lead was followed by numerous club members who helped in all sorts of ways. I can mention only Austen Deans and Morris White whose contributions were quite outstanding.

Outside the Club, David Lange and Mike Moore showed interest and support we could not have reasonably expected from such busy people. In Beijing Carl Worker performed wonders in communicating our requests to the Chinese Mountaineering Association. We named our climbing teams after our major sponsors. Perhaps Toyota (NZ) deserves a special mention for their product had to survive not only atrocious conditions but also Mr Chan's dare-devil driving. David Ellis of Fairydown was particularly helpful in providing the extremely specialised down-suits as well as other equipment, as were Tony Rika and the Hallmark and Great Outdoors teams.

The expedition could not have taken place without the help of the Chinese Mountaineering Association. There is a special bond between New Zealand and Chinese mountaineers. Perhaps it is accentuated by the fact that neither group can match the lavish expenditures of expeditions from other countries. This expedition owes a special debt to Liaison Officer 'Pinetree', interpreter 'James' and driver Mr Chan.

Below is a list of those individuals and companies who helped us. If it is not totally comprehensive I apologise: Alex Harvey Industries, Alliance Freezing Comp., Alpine Guides, Alpsports, Ampro Sales, Antarctic Products, Arthur Ellis & Co. Ltd (Fairydown), Aulsebrooks Ltd, Alan Berry, Butland Industries, Cadbury Schweppes Hudson Ltd, Cashel Clinic, Caxton Printing Works, Chinese Mountaineering Association, Collins Publishers, Comalco, Continental Foodstuffs, Jess Danby, Daylyte, Austen Deans, Neil Dearlove, Diamond Foods Ltd, Dominion Newspaper, Donaghys Industries, Dorlon Products, J.T. Edmonds Ltd, Ernest Adams Ltd, ETA Foods Ltd, Fisher & Paykel, Fleming & Co. Ltd, Forty Below, Fritschi, Glaxo New Zealand Ltd, Gordon & Gotch, The Great Outdoors Company, W. Gregg & Co. Ltd, Griffin & Sons Ltd, H & H Group, Hallmark International, Hertz, Roy Hieskel, Hodder & Stoughton Ltd, Holeproof Industries, Holes Rye Breads, Malcolm Hood, Neville Johnson, Johnson Wax NZ Ltd, Jones Brothers, JONS Meat Supplies, Knight Industries Ltd, Kodak, Koflach, Rt. Hon. David Lange, H. Leighton Hill, Levi Strauss NZ Ltd, Link Consultants, Lydiard Shoes, T.A. MacAlister, Macpac Wilderness, Marley, Hon. Mike Moore, Colin Monteath, Mountain Recreation, Mt

Cook Group, Multimedia Systems, W.T. Murray Ltd, Nevada Sport, New Zealand Alpine Club, New Zealand Army, New Zealand Co-operative Dairy Co., New Zealand Embassy (Beijing), New Zealand Industrial Gases, New Zealand Insurance, New Zealand Kiwifruit Authority, New Zealand Sugar Co. Ltd, Norski, Nylex NZ Ltd, Coyla Olliver, Terry O'Rawe, Graham Painter, Richard Pearson, Quality Packers Ltd, Qantas, Regina Confections, Remarkable Films, Rockgas, D.N. Russell & Co., Sanitarium Health Food Co., Scott Housewares, Seagram (NZ) Ltd, Sealord Products Ltd, Sew Hoy and Sons Ltd, Shipping Corporation of New Zealand, Signs & Plastic Products Ltd, Skellerup, Ski Industries (NZ) Ltd, Southland Development Corporation, J.K. Sparrow, Sporting Highlights, Sunshine Leisure, R.C. Supple, Southland Tramping Club, Tait Electronics, Taylors Engineering, TEMCO, Thomas Cook, Toyota (NZ), Ultralon Products, Union Carbide, Variety Travel Ltd, Vision Holdings Ltd, Waitaki NZ Refrigeration Co., Wakefield Metal, Watties Industries, Morris White, Wilkinson Sword Group, Bong Wong, Carl Worker, W.H. Worrall & Co., Alan Young and 3M.